EFFECT 12 30 AM CST EAST BOUND TRAINS. MONDAY JUNE 2 -1890

	FREIGHT TRAINS—Second Class.						STATIONS.	PASSENGER TRAINS—First Class.									STATIONS.
	NO. 92	NO. 88	NO. 26 Freight. Daily.	NO. 28 Freight. Daily.	NO. 30 Way Freight Daily exc't Sunday.	NO. 20 Freight. Daily.	NO. 22 Freight. Daily.		NO. 55 Chicago Express. Daily.	NO. 6 Limited Express. Daily.	NO. 10 Passenger. Daily exc'p Sunday.	NO. 8 Limited. Daily.	NO. 16 Passenger. Daily exc't Sunday.	NO. 4 Passenger. Daily.	NO. 46 Express. Daily exc'p Monday.	NO. 14 Passenger. Daily exc'p Sunday.		
	PM Lv	PM Lv	PM Lv	AM Lv	AM Lv	AM Lv	AM Lv		PM Lv	PM Lv	PM Lv	PM Lv	PM Lv	AM Lv	AM Lv	AM Lv		
	5 10	2.43		9.10	5.30			Sandusky			6.10		2.00	7.40				Sandusky
	5 13	2.50		9.13	5.35			L. S. & M. S. Crossing			6.15		2.02	7.42			0.2	L. S. & M. S. Crossing
	5.24	3.05		9.28	5.51			Perkins'			6.25		2.10	7.49			4.5	Perkins'
	5.41	3.17		9.40	6.04			Prout's			6.38		2.16	7.56			7.0	Prout's
	5.53	3.30		9.52	6.12			Higbee			6.38		2.21	8.01			10.4	Higbee
	6.12	3 48		10.11	6.29			Roby's Siding			6.46		2.29	8.09			13.1	Roby's Siding
	6 14	3.56		10.13	6.30/7.00			Monroeville		11.10	6.50/7.15		2.31	8.12			15.3	Monroeville
	6 20	4 05		10.27	7.16			Pontiac		11.18	7.23		2.38	8.19			19.0	Pontiac
	6 45	4 20		10.43	7.32			Havana		11.26	7.29		2.45	8.27			22.0	Havana
	10 02	4 35		10.59	7.48			Centerton		11 34	7.36		2.52	8.35			26.7	Centerton
	10.10/11.00	5.13/5.27	1.13	11 04/11.30	7.53/8.30	6.10	3.40	Chicago Junction		11.40	10.20	7.42/7.50	2.57	8.40/8.55	3.00	1.45	28.8	Chicago Junction
	11.31	5 46	1.56	11.40AM	8.42	6.28	3.53	New Haven			10 26	7.56	5.33	3.04	9.01	3.00	1.52	31.3	New Haven
	11.6	6.00	2.10	12.10AM	8.58/9.04	6.45	4.08	Plymouth			10.31	8.03	5.38	3.10	9.08	3.12	1.59	34.4	Plymouth
	12 01AM	6.15	2.21	12.30	9.25	6.59	4.10	Forest			10.36	8.10	5.43	3.16	9.14	3.23	2.06	37.6	Forest
	12.23	6 35	2.45	1.00/1.21	9.45	7.22/7.32	4.40	Shelby Junction			10.43	8.19	5.50	3 25	9.24	3.31	2.16	42.2	Shelby Junction
	12.28	6 37	2.50	1.21	9.55	7.35	4.43	Shelbytown			10.46	8.21	5.52	3.27	9.27	3.33	2.18	42.9	Shelbytown
	12 56	7 00	3.27/3.37	1.51	10 70/10.10	8.05	5.15	Spring Mill			10.55	8.33	6.02	3.37	9.40	3.43	2.30	49.0	Spring Mill
	1 11	7 25	4.00/4.10	2.09	10.55	8.23	5.33	North Siding			11.03	8.43	6.09	3.40	9.50	3.50	2.30	54.0	North Siding
	1.15	7 29	4.20	2.14	11.04	8.28	5.40	Mansfield			11.06	8.46	6.12	3.51	9.55	3.55	2.55	54.5	Mansfield
	1.19	7.33	4.45	2.10	11.28	8.56	6.10	Alta			11.15	9.00	6.20	4.00	10.05	4.03	3.04	58.5	Alta
	2 01	8 10	5.40	3.00	11 52AM	9.19	6.40/6.50	Lexington			11.21	9.10	6.26	4.10	10.19	4.09	3.12	62.7	Lexington
	2.22/2.32	8 31/8.41	5.30	3 30/3.50	12.22/12.37	9.45/10.22	7.10	Shaffer's Siding			11.27	9.21	6.32	4.18	10.22	4.15	3.20	67.0	Shaffer's Siding
	2 35	8 47	5.25	3.45	12.41	10.26	7.14	Belleville			11.28	9.23	6.33	4.19	10.24	4.16	3.22	68.2	Belleville
	2.45	8 55	5.34	3.57	12.51	10.35	7.21	Clover's			11.31	9.28	6.36	4.23	10.28	4.19	3.26	70.2	Clover's
	3 01	9.10	5.54	4.10/4.09	1.05	10.50	7.40	Independence			11.35	9.36	6.41	4.29	10.35	4.24	3.32	73.7	Independence
	3 31/3.11	9.27/9.17	6.20	5.00	1.30	11.18	8.06	Ankenytown			11.45	9.47	6.48	4.50	10.47	4.59	3.41	79.5	Ankenytown
	4.00	10.10	6 45/6.35	5.10	1.50	11.11/12.15	8.59	Frederick			11.49PM	9.57	6.55	4.40	10.57	4.36	3.49	81.1	Frederick
	4.05/5.05	10.13	7.10/8.00	5.44	2.53/3.15	1.50	9.07/9.17	Mt. Vernon			12.01AM	10.13	7.07	5.03	11.17	4.44	4.04	91.1	Mt. Vernon
	5.05	11 07	9 10/9.10	6 01	3.31	1.30	9.40	Hunt's			12.00	10.24	7.16	5.15	11.20	4 50	4.15	96.5	Hunt's
	5 21/3.31	11 27	9.33	6.21	3.51	2.10/2.50	10.05	Utica			12.17	10.35	7.24	5.25	11.44	5.05	4.20	102.4	Utica
	5.51	11 43	9 55	6.40	4.07	2.44	10.23	St. Louisville			12.24	10.44	7.31	5.34	11.53	5.12	4.36	107.3	St. Louisville
	6.05/6.15	11.55PM	10 07	6.50	4.17	2 55	10.33	Vanatta's			12.29	10.50	7.36	5.40	11.59AM	5.16	4.42	110.4	Vanatta's
	6 35	12 10AM	10.25	7.03	4 30	3.10	10.50	Kibler's Siding			12.35	10.59	7.42	5.47	12.07PM	5.22	4.50	114.4	Kibler's Siding
	6.40	12 13	10.30	7.19	4.35	3.15	10.55	Newark			12.40	11.05	7.47	5.50	12.10	5.25	4.55	115.8	Newark
	AM Ar	AM Ar	PM Ar	PM Ar	PM Ar	PM Ar	AM Ar			M Ar	AM Ar	PM Ar	PM Ar	PM Ar	PM Ar	AM Ar	AM Ar	
	NO. 92	NO. 88	NO. 26	NO. 28	NO. 30	NO. 20	NO. 22			NO. 55	NO. 6	NO. 10	No. 8	NO. 16	NO. 4	NO. 46	NO. 14	

Note important changes in train numbers and time of trains—also additional trains.

6-2-1890

B&O RR   SANDUSKY MANSFIELD AND NEWARK

LAKE to ERIE
STRAITSVILLE

SANDUSKY   MANSFIELD
and
NEWARK

NEWARK   SOMERSET
and
STRAITSVILLE

COLUMBUS   SHAWNEE
and
HOCKING

B&O

CARL T. WINEGARDNER

Table of Contents

Dedication ....

About the Author ....

In The Beginning ....

Portland (Sandusky City) Sandusky South ....

The Men of the Railway Post Office ....

Prout 1

Kimbal (Higbee) 1

Monroeville .... 1.

Havanna 1

Centerton 1

Chicago Junction (Willard) 1

Plymouth 2

Shelby (Shelbytown) 2

Mansfield 2

Lexington 2

Belleville 2

Butler 2

Ankenytown 2

Fredericktown (Frederick) 2

Mt. Vernon 3

Utica 3

St. Louisville 3

Newark 3

National Road 5

Thornville (Avondale) 5

Thornport 5

Glenford 58

Somerset 5

Junction City 6

Bristol 64

McCuneville 70

Rock Run 7

Old Straitsville (Hocking Valley) 7

Shawnee 7

New Straitsville 7

Ohio Mineral (Claycraft) 74

Columbus and others 72-8

Disasters on the Straitsville 8

The Central Ohio Railroad Bridge Collapse 8

Locust Grove Disaster 84

Newark, Ohio Incident (April 5th 1924) 8

Mt. Vernon Incident (September 6, 1955) 8

Last Train From Newark 88

This Book is Dedicated to:

All railroad employees that I have worked with on and for B&O Railroad.

First, there has to be, The History Collectors of Shawnee Perry County. Wes Tharp, Elaine Higgins, Jimmy Bath, Walter Harrop Collection, Perry County Historical Society, Elanor Shaefer of Glenford Pictures, Larry Parker, of New Lexington.

The many people I contacted; Ruth Courson of Thornville (I attended school, in the same grade, with her.), B&O Engineering Department, with pictures of all bridges on "The Straitsville ", B&O Historical Society Baltimore MD. and Smithsonian Institute of Washington D. C. (I belong to both) for suppling me with pictures and history.

Paul Dunn Collection of Zanesville, for taking and exchanging our photo's of B&O through the years (I was his #1 picture taking subject).

Licking County Historical Society for history and pictures, Bud Abbott and Chance Brockway Pictures.

Newark Library for securing history and Denison University Library, Earl Griffth for doing the microfilm reproduction.

The Newark Advocate for all the pictures and history that they record each day on micro film. Stefanei Clippinger, for all the help The Advocate gave me. B&O Steamers Unit at Newark for working with them.

Mt Vernon Knox County Historical Society.

Mt. Vernon Library for all the history and pictures of Knox County.

Fredericktown Historical Society.

Wendel Fink and their collection of Frederick and Ankeny Town.

Butler to Sandusky are from my collection - 1946 to 198'

Carl T. Winegardner

ISBN 0-9662353-0-4
$25.00

To Tom

Carl T Winegardner 1998

1

About the Author

I was born in the country, south of Thornville, Ohio in the year of 1924. I attended Perry County Schools. I went to first grade at a small country school called Bruno, where we had one teacher for eight grades of classes. I attended Thorn Township School at Thornville for the next 11 grades, and graduated in 1942.

I was raised on the farm during the Great Depression of the 1930's. There was very little money in our household. If you didn't raise or grow your food, you didn't eat. We lived through it and attended school. I was transported in 1931 REO bus from home-to Thornville. I will never forget the heating system. The exhaust entered a two inch pipe and ran on the floor through the bus. There was no thermostat to turn up the heat.

On December 7, 1941 - my senior year of high school - war was declared. Many Perry County boys entered the Service, and some never returned alive. I, for one, was part of the Naval Service and belonged for 34 years.

I entered service with the Baltimore & Ohio Railroad on December 26, 1944. I will never forget how I started with them. I arrived at Newark around 8:00am at the hiring room. The train master clerk said they were hiring brakemen and firemen. He sent me to the examining doctor for an exam. He passed me and I was sent to the crew dispatcher. He wanted me to be on the crew as a student brakeman and fireman helper. I went up town Newark to the JC Penney store and bought a railroad worker outfit. I had a sandwich and was at the caller office on time. Every one of the crew was older than my dad. Mind you, I had never seen or been on a steam locomotive. The closest I was to one was at the Route 13 crossing in Thornport, as the local went by.

Between railroad and Service, I stayed with them 44+ years. I worked trains all over the Newark Division. Sandusky Willard to Newark to Cincinnati to Wheeling, West Virginia to Parkersburg, West Virginia by the way of Zanesville, to Cumberland by Cambridge and the best Newark to Shawnee on the Straitsville.

I was head brakeman on the last train out of Shawnee to Newark. After we left they closed it down to Somerset from Shawnee.

Back to that first train ride. This had to be the largest machine I was ever on. We made it to Cincinnati and back to Newark, where I reported to the crew dispatcher. That trip was all the student runs I made. I was called for the same train I came in on. As the head brakeman to Benwood, West Virginia, this run was at night. The crew consisted of two engineers and two firemen, with a flagman and a conductor This was a double header train. They took good care of me. What a life this was. I had to learn railroad work quickly and safely. I fired and broke both jobs with those steam engines. The Unions stopped me from working both jobs, so I stayed with train service and was made a conductor in 1952.

The first trip that I was the conductor, we killed a man at Zanesville. The reports I had to fill out were something. The man was the same age as my father. This was not the last report I filled out. I filled out many in the following years.

I started taking pictures of the B&O in 1946. The camera I first had came from Belgium. It was a small type and used 00 film. There were six shots on a roll.

I worked everywhere. The years on the B&0. The best job I considered working was in passenger service in 1950's. The regular trains were long miles. Newark to Wheeling to Cincinnati to Newark - 530 miles on the trip.

I was the last promoted passenger conductor on the Newark Division. The highlight of this was that, as the conductor, I ran the National Limited from Midland City to Benwood, West Virginia.

All passenger trains on the Newark Division ended in July 1961. I worked freight trains all over the Division until I retired in 1989. After:: I retired I had all of these pictures, so I decided to write this book. It starts in Sandusky.

In the Beginning

At Portland around 1830, the Lake steamers were the only transportation of Ohio products that existed. The port built slips so ships could dock and take on cargo for Buffalo and the east. At that early day, immense freight wagons were doing the carring trade for the country.

Lake Erie was the state's largest outlet for grain and produce. Pork, wheat, whiskey furs and everything else then produced in Ohio were placed on wagons, where they made their slow way to Lake Erie.

Portland (Sandusky City) became a very important market for Ohioans. Large dock fronts were built on each side of the ships slips. Warehouses were later built to handle the freight. Around 1835 a few enterprising men conceived the idea to build a railroad from that point south. Around that time Portland became Sandusky City.

This movement threw the entire freight business from its southern terminal point. This was one of the first railroads to be built in Ohio. It was built and used before the steam engine.

When their railroad was first built, wooden rails were used as the cars were only small boxes on wooden wheels. These crude railcars were hauled and pulled by horses. The railroad started right down on the water front of Sandusky City and was built to Monroeville. It was not long until the steam powered locomotives superseded horse power. For quite a while after that, the road bed continued to be wooden, the cars ran on wooden rails which had been fastened to a piece of strap iron.

The wooden railroad has thus been described: "The construction of the roadbed was solid if a multiplicity of timbers could make it so. First a mud-sell was laid down length-wise of the road. Strong cross ties were then spiked on this mud-sill. Into these 'gains' were cut, and these received the wooden rails which were sawed to fit them."

These rails were about five inches wide at the top, broading at the bottom where they entered the gains, and were about seven inches high. On these, ribbon was spiked, being a strip of hard wood about two and a half inches wide by one inch thick, and on this the strap iron rail was laid Spikes were driven throughout the strap rail and the ribbon, into the large wooden rail beneath. The heads of the spikes, being sunk into the eyes in the strap rails, they left a smooth surface for the car wheels to run on. This railroad required three times the material of today's railroads. This is how the very first railroad was built.

On March 12, 1836 a charter was obtained for a road from Mansfield to New Haven. The building of their railroad interfered somewhat with the building of the first mentioned railroad. However, it soon turned out that neither was of great value without the cooperation of the other, so a plan was agreed upon to fill the gap between New Haven and Monroeville. This railroad was 54 miles between Mansfield and Sandusky City, therefore it was named the Mansfield and Sandusky City.

The Columbus and Lake Erie Railroad was chartered on March 12, 1845. This was Newark's first railroad, and it extended 62 1/2 miles from Newark to Mansfield. At this point it connected with the Mansfield and Sandusky. This opened a direct transportation line - Newark to Lake Erie.

On November 23, 1853 these two companies merged with a third that held the small Huron and Oxford Railroad. Hence, it came to be the Sandusky, Mansfield and Newark Railroad Company. The railroad was still wooden, so steel rails were laid around 1855, just before the Civil War.

South of Newark, in 1867, the Newark, Somerset and Straitsville was organized and built 44 miles south to Shawnee. It was built and arrived at Shawnee in 1871. However, at Rock Run the line was extended to Old Straitsville.

The railroads were changing from wood to coal for fuel for their many locomotives and other coal fired boilers. Perry County coal filled these many orders for coal. The Baltimore and Ohio Railroad had their own big mine on the Rock Run, known as #3 Mine.

Portland (Sandusky City) Sandusky South

From the 1889 time table the SM&N was running three passenger trains daily between Newark and Sandusky, one daily between Monroeville and Chicago Junction. Four ran between Chicago Junction and Newark. This made seven trains daily.

On the second class freight trains there were three Sandusky to Newark, and three Chicago Junction to Newark. This made six second class. There were many third class and extra trains.

The Passenger Depot was downtown and close to the Lake Erie water front. The railroad was built in the middle of Water Street and it serviced many industries. Most were large warehouses at which they handled the freight traffic between rail and ship.

At Sandusky City

After the railroad was built, it was powered by being pulled by horses. The first steam locomotive in Ohio arrived by ship from England at Sandusky City Harbor. This engine was built to Ohio gauge to match the railroad. It was fired by wood, and Lake Erie water was used for steam. It was a 2-4-0 built engine Cooper, and being the first locomotive in Ohio, it was named the "Sandusky."

Tauton Locomotive Works built the rest of the SM&N engines in the U.S. All were used on the SM&N into Newark and Columbus. All were made for 15 air condition, which meant they would go 15 miles per hour and 15 outside air. Hot in summer and cold in winter.

After the Baltimore and Ohio took control of the SM&N, 60 pound steel rails were laid and gauge was B&O type. In later years, heavier and more powerful engines were built, as well as bigger and larger freight cars. Then came the passenger trains. All were wooden built with oil lighting and wood and coal stoves for heat.

The railroads were granted right to start hauling U.S. Mail and Express. This meant another type of car had to be added to the train. Hence, the Mail and Baggage Car. This mail service came to be known as the U.S. Railway Postal Service. They picked up and delivered U.S. Mail at every station on the line they worked, transferring mail at the terminals where they arrived. Rural mail carriers were powered by the horse and buggy.

Then came Henry Ford's Model "T". On many railway post office cars there would be as many as five postal workers. They would post mark and cancel all mail with the train stamp. The following story explains how Americans got their mail by train.

THE MEN OF THE RAILWAY POST Office

The jobs in the Railway Mail Service were advertised as a way to travel the rails and enjoy the scenery in a relaxed and leisurely manner. In reality, the jobs allowed no time for enjoyment. Working on a Railway Post Office car required a special breed of mail clerk. Temperatures ranged from blistering hot in the summer to sub-freezing in the winter. The cars, especially the wooden ones, were deathtraps in a train wreck. The cars carried as many as 22 postal clerks and all the mail - sorted and unsorted.

In the earliest days of railroading, the U.S. Government considered the railroads too unreliable to carry the mail. It was not until November 1831, some five years after the first chartered railroad went into service, that the South Carolina Railroad first carried the U.S. Mail. On January 1, 1832, the Baltimore & Ohio began carrying mail between Frederick and Baltimore, Maryland. When the B&O opened a line between Washington, D.C., the railroad set aside a compartment specifically for the mail, but also for postal employees to sort it. And, by 1855, the Terre Haute & Richmond Railroad (eventually absorbed into the New York Central system) operated post office cars in which mail could be sorted en route.

Since no regulations existed to regulate rates, some railroads saw the federal government as an easy way to cover financial losses. Outrageous rates were charged for handing the mail - in one case, over $500 per mile. To secure lower rates, the mail clerks began riding as passengers with the mail carried as luggage in the baggage car. The railroads soon caught on, and began "losing" trunks of mail. Finally, by 1860, the government passed laws to regulate rates being charged to the postal service.

The U.S. Post Office created the Railway Mail Service in early 1864. The permanent Railway Post Office car (RPO), equipped to pick up, sort, and deliver mail en route, was placed in operation by Chicago and North Western Railway on August 28, 1864. This car, unlike earlier ones which were ad lib arrangements, was the first designed specifically to facilitate the sorting of mail. This first car was simply a baggage car with sorting counters and wooden "pigeon holes" installed. One of the clerks on this first RPO car was a young man by the name of Fred Harvey. He later founded the Fred Harvey Company, securing the dining car rights for the Atchison, Topeka and Santa Fe Railroad and establishing a chain of famous hotels and restaurants across the Southwest to cater to railroad passengers. The company still exists and is the major concessionaire of Grand Canyon National Park.

The Railway Mail Service made letters affordable to the average person. From 1825 to 1845, mailing a three page letter could cost up to 75 cents. In 1845, the rates were reduced to five cents per half-ounce if sent less than 300 miles and 10 cents over that distance. In 1851, rates dropped again, this time to three cents per half-ounce within 3,000 miles; six cents for greater distances. By 1885, first class postage cost only two cents per ounce no matter what distance. The efficiency of the RPO's had cut as much as 73 cents off the price of a letter. In 1932, the rates jumped back up to three cents per ounce. The rates stayed there until the 1960's and, by the time of the last RPO car run in 1977, had climbed to 13 cents per ounce.

To keep this nationwide network operating, over 25,000 men worked for the Railway Mail Service. They worked as station duty clerks, dumpers, sorters, pouch casers, and registry clerks.

The least experienced crew member was usually the dumper. He sorted the sacks of mail at the beginning of the trip into three categories. One group consisted of letters going straight through. These letters would not be sorted en route, merely dropped off at the end of the journey to be picked up by the next train. There were long range and even transcontinental letters. The second category was for mail transfers between different railway lines or RPO routes. The third group, the most important, was the mail for towns along the RPO's route. The through, transfer, and local pouches each were hung according to their disposition - transfer-or drop-off- and final destination.

Once these bags were hung in order, the dumper concentrated on emptying the arriving bags for sorters to process. He also ensured, under the direction of the pouch caser, that the station duty clerk received the proper bag at the proper time to toss out at a station. As mail bags were picked up "on the fly," the dumper emptied the bags for the sorters. This was strenuous work, requiring the strength to carry heavy mail bags from one end to the other while the train sped along at 50 to 80 miles-per-hour.

The most hazardous job on the RPO was that of station duty clerk - also called door duty. He had two duties. One was dropping off mail, the other picking up mail. Unfortunately, these duties had to be performed at the same time.

As the train approached the station at better than 50 miles-per-hour, the station duty clerk looked for his landmark. This might be a particular bridge, barn, house, or any other easily recognizable object. Visibility was often bad due to coal smoke, fog, rain, snow, or darkness. Even the landmarks might change. One clerk on door duty was looking for a "big, old weather beaten barn." He sailed past the drop point and complained, "I'll be they painted the go-darn barn." In the days of steam, he also had to dodge the occasional piece of coal falling from the tender while searching for the elusive landmarks. When he spotted the landmark, he knew approximately how much time until the drop point.

After the train passed the landmark, the clerk readied himself for the drop and pickup. The dumper passed him the bag of mail for that station. The station duty clerk placed the bag on his foot and opened the door on the side of the RPO. He adjusted his goggles, leaned out into the biting wind, and watched for the mail pouch hanging on the mail crane. As the train approached the mail pouch, he extended the catcher arm. This V shaped iron bar was designed to hook the mail pouch from the crane as the train sped by. When the hook hit the pouch, it grabbed the bag and pulled it alongside the car. As soon as it was within reach, the door duty clerk grabbed hold, pulled it inside, and tossed it to the dumper. The clerk had to be careful. If he lifted the catcher arm out too soon, it might hit a boxcar parked on a siding. A fraction of a second too late and he might miss the mailbag altogether. One clerk missed five mail cranes in a row. When the train stopped at a large station, the supervisor began berating the man for his carelessness. At this point, the engineer poked his head in the side door to apologize for knocking down all the mail bags. One of the grabirons on the engine was bent at exactly the right height to hit the cranes.

While the station duty clerk tried to hook the bag from the mail crane, he also made the delivery. As his aiming point arrived, he kicked the delivery bag out the door, hoping no unsuspecting bystander was in the way. If he kicked the bag too hard, it might go through the station window. Not hard enough, it might get sucked under the wheels where letters, checks, money orders, and packages would be shredded. If he kicked it out too soon or too late, who knew what it might hit. One clerk on the Milwaukee Road lost his shoe while booting the pouch out. Without missing a beat, he kicked off his other shoe so whoever found them would have a pair.

The sorter's job was to sort all mail entering the car - either before leaving the yard, or underway. Before the train left the station at the beginning of the trip, the sorters had to deal with all unsorted mail. This mail came directly from the local post office, which separated the mail only by RPO route - not by drop point. Once on the train, it was sorted by drop point, transfer point, or put into the through mail pouch.

The drop point mail was sorted by each community's station. Each station had its own pigeon hole, small wooden boxes stacked above the sorting table with the name of the town written on them. Not all of the pigeon holes were for towns on the train's route. Large cities or towns usually receiving large batches of mail also had their own boxes. After the train started its journey, they sorted each new batch of mail coming into the RPO. There was a certain amount of pride involved with sorting the mail. If a crew finished the trip with unprocessed mail, this reflected badly on the sorters.

Transfer point mail also required quick, efficient handling. These letters and packages, destined for towns on another RPO's route, had to be ready before the transfer point arrived. Sorting the mail received at the transfer was as important as sorting the new batches from the stations. Some of the mail might carry an address for the next stop.

The through mail was the simplest. Ignored through the trip, it only became important at the end. Each bag of through mail was for a specific location. Any mail for that location, previously sorted into pigeon holes, went into the bag. This required a thorough knowledge of geography. Sorting for major cities like Baltimore, Boston, or even Scranton was not difficult. But it required detailed knowledge to know, for example, that a letter to Towson went to Baltimore. Imagine working an RPO in Kentucky and seeing a letter addressed to Throop or Moosic. Obviously, they could not know every little town in the country, but time was wasted when mail clerks had to look up the location of a community.

The most important clerk on board was the pouch caser. He decided which pouch of mail was sorted when. If the pouches were sorted in the wrong order, mail for an approaching drop-off might not be ready. He also prepared transfer pouches which required intimate knowledge of the scheduled and routes of all RPO's so a letter or package reached its destination with minimal delay. The pouch caser was also responsible for verifying that the postage was correct and applying the cancellation. He swiftly switched from one pile to another, canceling all letters before the drop point arrived.

Lady, the registry clerk handled all special mail, such as payroll and treasury shipments, (two reasons why RPO clerks were armed), bank transfers, jewelry and over valuable cargo. He kept records, in triplicate, for the special mail, including all insured, registered or certified mail, keeping careful track of incoming and outgoing. If the incoming did not equal outgoing at the end of the trip, he could, theoretically, be held personally responsible for the lost mail. This was a coveted position, usually held by a senior clerk. Benefits included a fair amount of free time and comparatively moderate physical demands.

Boredom was never a problem, thought alertness was. The clerks worked 10 hour days in difficult conditions. A clerk with a spare moment, usually the registry clerk, brewed "mail lock coffee." If a heavy mail lock floated in it, or, according to some, it if dissolved, the coffee was strong enough to drink. This lethal brew, paired with cold sandwiches, provided sustenance on the long journeys.

The Railway Post Office Car at Steamtown National Historic Site was operated on the Louisville and Nashville Railroad. This line operated between St. Louis, Missouri and Cincinnati, Ohio in the North and New Orleans, Louisiana and Augusta, Georgia in the South. It also went as far East as Norton, Virginia.

The L&N acquired its first all-steel RPO's in 1913 from American Car and Foundry. They were heavy duty cars with six-wheel trucks. The cars carried the numbers 1100 through 1104. An interesting feature in these cars was the rotating label boards for the pigeon holes, allowing the car to operate on four different RPO routes.

After car #1100 was acquired by Steamtown USA in 1977, it was used for demonstrations, including picking up the mail "on the fly" in Bellows Falls, Vermont. After Steamtown USA moved to Scranton, Pennsylvania, they painted the car in the livery of the Delaware, Lackawanna, and Western Railroad, even though it never served on that road.

This beautifully maintained car is a fitting tribute to the men who served long hours in brutal conditions sorting and delivering the mail. Today, we can appreciate the quality construction of the car. It is preserved as a reminder to those who received mail via the RPO system, a testimony to the mail crews who worked for them. It also provided an opportunity for the visitor to view the inside of a forbidden car - only Railway Mail Service personnel were allowed inside the car when it was in operation. We use it as an interpretive tool, helping tell an important part of American history.

United States Department of the Interior

NATIONAL PARK SERVICE
Steamtown National Historic Site
150 South Washington Avenue
Scranton, Pennsylvania 18503-2018

IN REPLY REFER TO:

H14

February 16, 1994

Mr. Carl T. Winegardner
1224 Nadine Drive
Heath, Ohio 43056

Dear Mr. Winegardner:

Your interview has been deposited in the Steamtown National Historic Site library. I have enclosed your copy of the release form and the interview.

Thank you for contributing to the Steamtown Oral History Project.

Sincerely,

Mark Morgan
Historian

Water Street, Sandusky

At this location was the very first start of the railroad south. Notice that there are three tracks. Here is where the freight was unloaded first by wagon trains, then railroad cars.

Lake Erie in Background

These are the piers where freight was transferred to the ships. Notice the slips on both sides for the ships to dock. This is the slip where the Lake Erie Steamers docked and then exchanged cargo. The wharf looks today as it did in the 1800's. There were coal loading facilities and slips east of this one. They also loaded limestone and gravel. Paper making companies in later years moved into these large warehouses. The railroad operation at Sandusky was a seven day, 24 hour operation. Many a car of Perry County coal made it to Sandusky.

Lake Erie.

Westvaco, one of the large warehouses built to handle lake freight, ship slip on right.

Sandusky Warehouses
This one was the first built to handle rail freight in and out from the ships. Notice the slip on the right.

B&O and NYC SM.N - LS&MS Crossover Diamond.

LS&MS (NYC) home signal, Rt. 250 and Rt. 13 under pass.

Lake Erie
The last rail car spotted in warehouse is as far north as the rail went.

Perkins Yard   Perkins Avenue

Sandusky City Yards

There was much industry that was built here. There were three railroads that serviced them. Here is where the SM&N crossed the (NYC) LS & MS. The transfer track is just west of this crossing. Later it was New York Central Low Level Line. On this route ran the 20th Century limited passenger train between New York City and Chicago.

Perkins Yard

Perkins Yard M.P.4.5 This was B&O inbound and out bound yard. All freight from and to entered Perkins Yard. Also interchanged cars from the "Central" at the transfer track. For the size of the yard and the storage tracks, it handled many trains in and out in 24 hours. Around Perkins district there was much industry that required switching. Here was the main yard where all north bound freight trains entered. There were 10 tracks plus the LS & MS transfer track.

Wagner Quarry

Wilmer MP 6 This spur was one mile long, and it serviced Wagner Quarries and Soldiers Sailors Home. Wagner Quarry loaded limestone for the railroad, which used it for ballast under the rails. On the average day, they shipped 20 cars. The B&O received railroad ballast stone here. Wagner shipped out around 20 loads per day. There is Wagner stone on the Straitsville.

Prout Junction

Prout Junction MP 7.6 This was a large grain and seed station that loaded corn, wheat and beans out by the car load. Prout Junction Switch was on a curve and a bank west. When a Lake Erie snow drifted the cut, this is what it looked like. 15 feet of drifted snow stalled many a train. Prout was made into an industrial track to service a large grain center and tank farm.

Prout Curve in Winter

Notice the tank cars spotted in the snow. This is a Lake Erie snow. The drifts were around 10 feet high. In the background is the Ohio Turnpike.

Kimball

Where the B&O crossed the NYCST NICKEL PLATE. Two track transfer just south of crossing. Right of Engine 305. Here is Cedar Point. Excursion returning 1700 Westinghouse employees to Mansfield. Snow north of Monroeville.

Kimball, Ohio

Higbee (Kimball) MP 10.4 Crossed the "NICKEL PLATE" NYC & STL Railroad. Also transferred cars at their interchange track. Handled Way freight from the load to the Depot Building.

Monroeville

Transferred cars with the Wheeling and Lake Erie here. There were many cars in and out of here. Feed and grain were handled here. Passenger Depot with Engine 390 Agent was located here. LS & MS also ran through here.

Monroeville Roby's Siding MP 15.1

This was used as a passing sending and run around for the Chicago Junction passenger train. The depot was at the crossover of the Wheeling and Lake Erie Railroad. B&O Agent was on duty 24 hours a day. There was a great deal of interchange cars and grain elevator and feed mill. Also interchanged with the Michigan Central as a copy of the Way bill states. A car load of coal in 1880 weighed 14 1/2 tons.

Monroeville MP 15.3 Transfer to Michigan Central tracks was south of Wheeling and Lake Erie crossover. The feed mill was known as Seaman McLean. They processed feed at this mill. Grain was shipped in and processed, then it was shipped out by rail. The agent at this station was a very busy person. He was also the operator for the train orders.

Waybill for a car load of coal from Scotts Mine, Cambridge to Michigan Central Railroad, September 22, 1880. Transfer to Michigan Central.

Pontiac MP 19.0
This was a long grade out of Monroeville, and many a train needed a helper on the hill to Havana. All of these small stations on the Sandusky had a passenger shed where the people could board the trains either south to Chicago Junction or Newark, or north to Sandusky.

Havana MP 22
Here at Havana there was a passing siding on the west side and a large grain elevator on the east side, which did a considerable amount of trade. An agent operator was stationed here at the depot and handled express and passengers. North of Havana Station there was a straight piece of track that was flat surface. In the winter it would snow and drift. Many times the drifts would be four feet deep.

Havanna The track on right, passing siding on left. Depot was in background. This elevator handled a tremendous amount of grain shipped by rail.

Centerton MP 26.7
This was a small station which included a small depot and a grain elevator spur track. It was also the last station before Chicago Junction. Depot was located just past mill at road crossing.

Chicago Junction (Willard) MP 28.8
Chicago Junction was the main line yard and handled all trains. Engines were serviced and coaled and watered there. It was a mammoth lay out. Westbound received and Hump outbound. Eastbound received and Hump outbound also switched the Newark and Sandusky trains. Here is where 90% of the Shawnee coal went for company fuel. One could board westbound trains for Chicago, Illinois or for the east to Baltimore, Washington or New York City.

Chicago Junction East to Newark Leaving the depot with orders from the agent and operator, heading east or south as Newark Division was. Crossed the main street, Myrtle Avenue; and entered the Hill Track Yards. Here is where freight cars were set off from Newark and picked up for the Sandusky. It had a livestock resting station pens where livestock was rested and fed before continuing on their way to slaughter.

Chicago Junction Willard The SM&N ran through Chicago Junction to Sandusky before the terminal was built. The hill yards was the terminal. Then came the building of the large railroad yard. The yard was abut one mile wide and five miles long. Was the Chicago, Detroit, Toledo, Cincinnati, Lima, and all points west, freight and passenger trains to east. From the east came freight and passengers from New York, Washington, and all points west.

This was and still is one big operation. There was a coal tipple built to coal the steam engines in and out of the terminal. On the average, there were around 10 cars of coal consumed each day. Where did the coal come from? Perry County, Guernsey and Belmont. After the yards were built, the railroad built a large YMCA to house the train crews in and out of the terminal. There were the Chicago, Toledo, and Willard Terminal crews. Then came the New Castle, Cleveland, Lorain, and Wheeling. Then the Newark, Ohio. Willard was made a terminal for all these divisions. They operated all freight and passenger trains seven days a week, 24 hours a day, and all holidays. There was no down time whatsoever.

The B&O had a passenger train, the Capital Limited. It was strictly first class. No B&O employee - only the train crew - was allowed to ride it, except to pay first class fare. No passes. Movie stars from Hollywood rode this train, as did all high profile people.

All of the freight and passengers from the west routed B&O came through Chicago and Willard. Many a train entered and departed this terminal for points everywhere. To this day it is still a main line terminal.

B90 Westbound passenger train for Chicago. (1947)

Depot 1902

Depot 1930

NewHaven MP 31.3
This was a long passing siding where all Newark, Sandusky trains entered to clear the main track.

Plymouth MP 34.4
Plymouth, for it's size, was an industrial site. The B&O (SM&N) and Akron, Canton and Youngstown both had passenger depots with agents and clerks. Both railroads serviced the large Fate Root Heath Company, also with a transfer track. Here at this complex they had their own foundry, which required sand limestone, pig iron and railroad transportation in and out. Silver King farm tractors, Plymouth Industrial Locomotives and fork lifts were made here. Plymouth engines were built here. Stock pens were built here for livestock shipment in and out. Grain elevators were built at railroad sidings.

The Silver King farm tractor was the first tractor built with a single front wheel. I do not believe any other farm tractor company followed with the single wheel. Throughout the years, Plymouth did prosper through the railroad and their service. At the ACY Crossing there was a target for crossing protection. Horizontal for SM&N and vertical for ACY.

In the start of the railroad crossing here, there was a clerk operator station, and he handled the operation, plus train orders.

The Plymouth Passing siding was just east of the ACY. Here many a train meet was made. Trains northbound for Chicago Junction yard had to clear and hold here on account the yard was unable to take their train in, and also to clear the main for passenger trains.

Shelby Junction MP 42.2

Here is where the New York Central crossed and was known as the Big Four. Passenger depot was located at the Diamond and a large interchange tracks. Eastbound B&O passing siding was located north of NYC and westbound siding located south of NYC. Cars were interchanged here. There was agent operator at tower who handled all switches through interlocking.

Shelby The railroad (B&O) depot was located by Main Street. Here is where the agent was housed who handled all the paper work for the railroad. There was a great deal of railroad transportation here. The New York Central crossed at Big Four Junction. They had a passenger station and a large transfer and freight house, and transferred freight here and transferred freight with the B&O here.

At Shelby Junction, the eastward passing siding was north of the NYC and the westbound siding was just east and connected to the transfer tracks. All movement in and out of the junction was controlled by the NYC operator. There were many manufacturing plants here, and practically all had railroad spurs.

They had their own electric plant, which was fired by coal, and an unloading track where they could unload five cars at once. All coal came by rail.

Shelby Sales book was located just east of B&O depot, and paper was transported here to make all kinds of books.

Spring Mill MP 49 A passing siding was located here and a passenger shed was at Spring Mill Road. There was an electric railroad that ran between Mansfield and Shelby. Both used this depot shed.

Forest MP 37.6
Had a passenger shed and received U.S. Mail, as did all stations. They sent and received all U.S. Mail and express by railroad.

Conductor A.H. Nethers

Flagman "C.T." Winegardner

North Siding 54.0 B&O and SM&N yards were located here. There was an eastbound passing siding and a westbound passing siding. Here was where all Mansfield area cars were set off and picked up. Steel Mills, Brass Works and appliances were manufactured here. Was also a terminal for turnaround trains. Coal and water station.

Mansfield Main Street 1947

Looking North on left transfer at PRR crossover.

PRR Pensy transfer tracks, Main street Rt. 14.
Erie crossover on right, Mansfield, Ohio.

Mansfield Depot, Erie Railroad in background.

Mansfield MP 54.5 The B&O Depot was located just east of the Erie Railroad crossing. It was built with cream colored brick, and I believe they came from Claycraft at Shawnee. The agent took care of all passenger trains and all freight business. The B&O had yard engines here, and all Mansfield work was done at north siding and controlled by the yard master and operator clerk.

A large steel mill, Empire Reeves, was serviced by the railroad B&O and PRR Pennsy. Scrap iron by the car load entered here for melting.

A mammoth grain elevator was built at the PRR and B&O Junction, and was serviced by both railroads through transfer tracks. Erie Railroad also went through Mansfield and did passenger and freight business with both B&O and PRR. B&O crossed both the Erie and PRR here. Many delays were made here while waiting for permission to cross.

Leaving Mansfield east, you start upgrade at the depot and continue up to Alta. Many trains got hung up on this grade and had to double to Alta passing siding.

North Butler

Butler

Butler

Ankenytown Station sign held by Wendel Fink

Independence (Butler) MP 73.7 Westbound and eastbound passing sidings and water station. Depot with agent and operator who handled the business of passenger trains, U.S. Mail Express and freight orders. A team track which handled storage cars and serviced a grain elevator. A lumber yard was at the north end of the track.

Ankenytown MP 70.5 Passing siding and team track which serviced a grain elevator. When the first trains started through here, the local people threatened to shoot the engine because it put out a squealing sound of the whistle when it approached the main crossing.

Alta MP 58.5

At Alta, which was the tallest peak on the SM&N at sea level, you had the Mansfield hill to climb coming east, and the Alta hill to climb going north. At Alta, there was a long passing siding and a WYE track connected at the east end. Helper engines turned here before returning east toward Newark. There was a long team track that serviced a coal company, lumber yard and green house. All did great railroad business.

Lexington MP 62.7

Passing siding, passenger depot with agent operator. Two grain elevators and industry were located here. They did a considerable amount of freight business.

Shaeffer's Siding MP 67.6

Passing siding was located here just north of Belleville.

Belleville MP 68.2

A team track and spur track were located here. Grain elevator and Foundry were here. Rt. 13 crossed the B&O here. Depot was just north of RT. 13. Agent was stationed here. Handled U.S. Mail

Lockhart MP 70

A passing siding was located here.

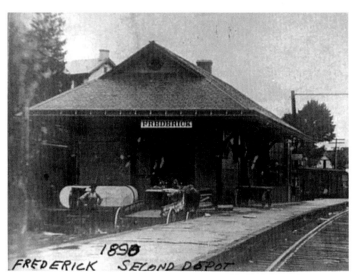

1890 Frederick, Second Depot.

North Team Track, Frederick, Ohio

Frederick (Fredericktown) MP 84.1

Frederick was a very busy rail head. To the north side was the stock team tracks. Here there were stock loading pens, coal and gravel unloading, and company storage materials. Today it is the rural farm district of farm supplies.

The first depot was built south of road crossing at the bridge. Was also used with grain elevator. Was built in the 1870's. SM&N train in Frederick in 1872. Notice the dam at the bridge. The second depot was built in the late 1800's with the Frederick name.

SM&N Northbound Freight 1872, Frederick, Ohio.

Large elevator was built to and continued north to the North Road crossing. The elevator was known later on as Updike. The team track handled coal, road tar tank cars, and material for the J.T. Foot Foundry. Logs were loaded here for shipment to the lumber yards. Many car loads of wheat and corn left this station. The depot was a passenger station and Express station. All of the daily needs came by rail. South end of Frederick was a coal unloading spur on west side and Sun glow Industries on east side. Sun Glow did tremendous rail business. They had their own foundry which all raw material came by rail. Their finished product was shipped by rail.

There were two major train wrecks at Frederick. The first was a head end collision 1895. Both engines came together in front of the depot. The southbound train was a freight and the northbound was a passenger train. The cause was, back then trains operated by time card time. All freight trains had to clear the main for passenger. This freight train ran out of time before he could clear Knox siding. The second was September 21, 1912. The following is from the Mt. Vernon Daily Banner.

B&O wreck,
Fredericktown, Ohio Sept.
21st, 1912.

Head end collision in front of Frederick Depot. 1895
SM&N South bound freight and North bound
passenger

Fredericktown Train Wreck
September 21, 1912

Seven freight cars on the B&O crashed into an embankment and were thrown into Kokosing River, and a large amount of their contents destroyed. The wreck occurred at 5:00am. A draw bar dropped out of one of the cars and caused the derailment. No one was injured. The train was a merchandise train and was traveling east at a good rate of speed. Several telegraph poles were knocked down and several small buildings damaged. Three cars rolled into the river, along with their contents of salt, chopped feed and pig iron. Only the iron can be recovered. Wreck train from Newark was re-railing the cars. While dragging one of the cars, it struck a large gas main and cut it in two. It was repaired in due time, and there was no fire.

The wreck was the cause of a long delay in traffic, with several trains being blocked. An east bound passenger train due in Mt. Vernon at 7: 10, and two west bound trains due at 8:26 and 8:57 were held until 12:00 noon before the Wreck ~train opened the track for service.

Frederick first Depot and elevator 1868

Frederick second Depot 1890

J.B. Foote Foundry Co.

J.B. Foote Foundry Co.

The last steam engine to switch Fredericktown was in Winter 1959. The last passenger train through Fredericktown south to Newark was train 246 around 6:00am on June 30, 1961. It went through to Wheeling, West Virginia, then in the evening, the last passenger train left Wheeling, West Virginia as no. 245. Extra cars were added at Wheeling for all the people that were to ride the last train. Some only rode station to station. I was a rider of this train as well. Gone was passenger train travel forever. The depot was sold and dismantled and moved to Wooster, as this picture states.

Last steam engine (#389) to switch
Fredericktown, 1959

Last run of the B&O 246 South
June 30, 1961, 6:00 a.m.

Knox Siding, Fredericktown, Ohio

Sun Glow Industries

Now, Fredericktown can boast about being the home of the FFA jacket. In 1935 there was an FFA farmer member going to Kansas City for the National Farmer Convention. He was a popular farmer from the area. A band was going along from the school, and they all wore the Fredericktown FFA jackets. The jackets were a hit at the convention and were endorsed at the FFA jacket nation wide. Their instructor was a person by the name of Grant. So became Fredericktown, home of the FFA jacket.

Knox Siding MP 85 At Knox, was located along passing siding. Was just south of Fredericktown. There was no water station, and the nearest restaurant was at Fredericktown. This was the ideal siding to hide a freight train for the train dispatcher. And believe you, trains crews were stuck here for hours meeting trains.

29

1950 billboard proclaiming Mt. Vernon as "Heart of Ohio"

Loading rail cars with drilling equipment. B&O siding at Gambier and Vine at South Norton, Mt. Vernon, Ohio

First CA&C train on new railroad, 1871 Mt. Vernon, Ohio

An early Cooper traction engine and Cooper separator provide the machinery for this Ohio scene in 1886.

One of the company's early portable steam engines, manufactured in 1870.

Cooper Bessemer of Mt. Vernon

It started in Mt. Vernon in 1833 with the advent of two brothers with an idea, a team of horses and the capital they had raised by the sale of a third horse. When Charles and Elias Cooper started their first foundry, they made plows, carding machines and similar simple machinery.

Charles and Elias Cooper came to Mt. Vernon from Zanesville in the Fall of 1833, hauling all they had in two wagons, and with their capital consisting of proceeds from the above mentioned horse. They built their first cupola blower as a primitive affair, driven by one (actual) horse power and with gear wheel made of wood. Charles Cooper told in later years how their first melt was made the following spring, and it took them all afternoon to make 500 to 700 pounds of castings.

The single horse "Bessie" continued to provide power until 1836 when they installed a small engine. Their inventions were as follows:

1836 - Small gas engine
1852 - First blowing machine with one steam and two air cylinders. It made 90 H.P. with three pounds of pressure.
1853 - Built the first steam locomotive west of the Alleghenies. It used wood for fuel and water for steam. Baltimore and Ohio Railroad used these engines for many years.
1857 - First self-propelled steam engine. Used horses to pull. Steering it had not been invented yet. Were used to power farm equipment or separators back then.
1869 - The Corliss Engine started, then became a Cooper main line product by 1886. They were made for 20 years.
1920 - Gas engines for pipe lines, then gasoline plants and the oil industry.

Large compressors were invented in the 1920's and were shipped all over the world. They were made in Mt. Vernon and shipped out by B~O Railroad. Today "Cooper" is a trade name and manufactures many products.

The Cooper name is the oldest plant name in Mt. Vernon, founded in 1833 and still going.

B&O Mt. Vernon Depot

The Mt. Vernon Bridge Company, builders of highway and railroad bridges

C.J. Cooper cane mill, 1863.

September 6, 1955 was a member of B&O Lake Erie Local, switching rail cars at Mt. Vernon. We were in Cooper Bessemer weighing a car of scrap paper. When we were leaving and I was closing the gate, there was a explosion at the test building about 300 feet from me. I was blown backward about 10 feet against the chain link fence. I was only slightly injured. The east wall of the testing building was totally blown out. Three men were killed at once. I believe lady luck was with us because the scale was located about 50 feet from that test building.

The crew of this local train was as follows:

Richard Forbes - Engineer E. Merle Henry - Fireman
Edward G. Welch - Conductor B. Morgan - Flagman
Carl T. Winegarnder - Head Brakeman

Mt. Vernon MP 91 The SM&N (B&O) through Mt. Vernon is part of the oldest railroad in Ohio. The oldest is part of the Lake Erie between Sandusky and Monroeville. The SM&N came through Mt. Vernon in the early 1850's.

Industry came on the heels of the railroad. First to build was C.B. Cooper, maker of steam powered farm machinery. Later on it became Cooper Bessemer, the giant builder of gas compressors for the fuel industry. They built their first wood fired steam locomotive in 1853, known as the Cooper Locomotive. They built their first diesel engine in the late 30's.

The next large industry was the Mt. Vernon Bridge Company. They built highway and railroad bridges. All were shipped by rail car. Shellman-Bettner, division of Continental Can Company, made the first plastic wrappers for Wrigley Brothers Chewing Gum of Chicago.

Northwestern Elevator and Mill Company processed farm livestock feed and shipped grain. Mt. Vernon Farmers Exchange handled grain and shipped many box cars of wheat. All grain loaded on the B&O at Mt. Vernon had to be weighed at Cooper-Bessemer Scales. In the grain season, this required many a rail switch - empty's in and loads out. The industries were Mt. Vernon Ice Delivery Company, Schlariet Transfer Company, Livestock pens for livestock shipping in and out, Texas Oil Company, O.C. Adleman, Standard Oil, Knox Chemical. S. Buchsbaum was a large buyer of livestock.

Pennsy Railroad (PRR) also came through Mt. Vernon. They switched the Pittsburgh Plate Glass and Chattanooga Glass. Both PRR and B&O had the best looking passenger station in the state. Passenger trains stopped here. In the 1916-1917 period, the Pennsy ran 12 trains, and the B&O ran six trains. All were daily. The last passenger train through Mt. Vernon was westbound B&O No. 245, June 30, 1961.

Memorial to Daniel Decatur Emmett,
composer of the song "Dixie", was a Mt. Vernon resident.

One of the last P6's - 5241 on train 246 in passing siding for
No. 95 Freight, Utica, Ohio. Earl Hartman, fireman.

B&O depot restored by the Utica
Sertoma, Utica, Ohio

Hunt MP 96.5

A long passing siding located here, as was freight house for local use. Was passenger train stop, flag stop. Rt. 13 crossed the B&O south of Hunt Station. Just north of Utica, the Buckeye Pipe Line loaded crude oil in tank cars for the oil refineries.

Utica MP 102.4

Utica, for its size, did a tremendous rail business. The main businesses were Ohio Tar & Asphalt, The Smith Wolf Oil Company, Weber and Weiss Coal Company, Lewis Branstool Elevator, Utica Coal Company. The Miller Company, maker of lighting equipment, was at near east side. Utica had two team tracks for loading and unloading material of all kinds. A passing siding was located here, and many trains met each other. The agent operator handled all rail business, including passenger trains between VanAtta and Mt. Vernon.

Central Ohio Rail Road.

NOTICE is hereby given that, in pursuance of the provisions of the Act entitled "An Act to incorporate the Central Ohio Rail Road Company," Books for subscription to the Capital Stock of said Company, will be opened on

Thursday and Friday, the 29th and 30th days of July inst.,

and remain open from 10 o'clock A M to 4 o'clock P M of each day, at the following places and under the direction of the following named Commissioners, or any three of them, to-wit: in the city of COLUMBUS, at the office of Alexander Patton, Esq., Mayor of said city—Commissioners, Messrs Joseph Ridgway, Bela Latham, Samuel Medary and Robert Neil: in the town of NEWARK, at the Banking office of A. J. Smith, Esq—Commissioners, Messrs Israel Dille, A. J. Smith, Jonathan Taylor and Dan'l. Duncan: in the town of ZANESVILLE, at the office of the County Auditor—Commissioners, Messrs D. Convers, Solomon Sturges, Robert Mitchell, James Raguet and Daniel Brush.

The object of such subscriptions will be, in pursuance of the Act as aforesaid, to organize the Central Ohio Rail Road Company.

JONA. TAYLOR.
DANIEL CONVERS,
JOHN HAMM.
JAMES RAGUET,
ROBERT MITCHELL,
LEVI CLAYPOOL,
W. CONDIT,
ROBT. NEIL,
I. DILLE,
GEO. W. PENNEY,
N. B. HOGG.

Dated July 1, 1847   42td

Central Ohio railroad notice.

Central Ohio Railroad Company stock certificate.

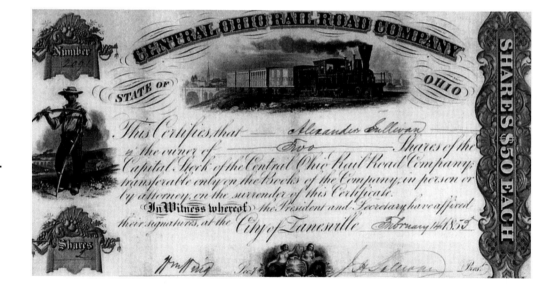

St. Louisville MP 110.4
A small passenger depot, which was a flag stop and a grain elevator, were the only business here.

Kibler MP 114.4
West end of double track ended here at the operator's tower. There were team tracks located here. Some were Ohio Power, Newark Water Works, Pure Oil Company, Socony Vacuum Company. The rest of the industry south will be shown in Newark Terminal.

B&O depot, Newark, Ohio. This was the last photo I took of the depot. It was set on fire and burned down in August, 1989.

Newark Terminal Around 1848, one of the greatest events in the history of the city of Newark was the finishing of The Columbus and Lake Erie to Newark.

The building of this road had been agitated for nearly 20 years. As early as 1834, meetings were held by the citizens of Licking County for the purpose of organizing such a railway and to at least obtain a survey of the route.

It was a mighty undertaking, however the county was yet sparsely settled, and the people too poor to engage in such an enterprise. However, since such conditions existed, in order to increase the growth and population, a charter was finally obtained. It was March 12, 1845 and this was Newark's first railroad. It extended 62.5 miles - Newark to Mansfield. Here it connected with Mansfield and Sandusky, thus opening a direct route to Lake Erie Port of Sandusky. This was the railroad known as the Sandusky Mansfield and Newark.

The railroad yard was at St. Clair street, and it was known as the St. Clair Yard. The picture is the first locomotive to arrive in Newark.

The second railroad to favor Newark with its presence was the Central Ohio. It came on right on the heels of the Sandusky Mansfield and Newark, having finished to Newark in 1854. The charter for the building of this road was granted on February 8, 1847, to run from Columbus, Ohio through Newark and Zanesville to such a point on the Ohio River as the directors might select.

The work on the portion of road between Columbus and Newark was commenced in June, 1850. Columbus and Lake Erie trackage was used Columbus to Newark. Those were hard times, however, for building railroads. The economy was in a slump and money was very difficult for the railroad to raise. The new road labored continually under financial embarrassment. In fact, before it could be finished, railway was placed in the hands of a receiver and in that condition operated until its final sale and reorganization in 1865. By teams of the reorganization, concessions were made by all classes of creditors and stockholders, by whom nearly four million dollars and stock and loans were sunk into the railroad.

The railroad ran easterly from Columbus through Newark, to the Ohio River at Bellaire, a distance of 137 miles. On November 21, 1866 the company reorganized and entered an agreement to be taken over and operated by Baltimore and Ohio. In February 1869, the Sandusky Mansfield and Newark was leased to Central Ohio for 17 years. They operated with B&O control the Lake Erie Division.

South of Newark, the Newark Somerset and Straitsville Railroad had been organized in 1867 and built 44 miles south to Shawnee by 1871. This line was leased by the Sandusky Mansfield and Newark on January 1, 1872 for 14 years, and to be equipped and operated by Baltimore and Ohio.

Depot and baggage building, Newark, Ohio. Both were destroyed in August 1989.

The last railroad to come to Newark was the Pittsburgh Columbus and Cincinnati Railroad. It was called the "Panhandle Route," named for the narrow section of West Virginia extending up and along the Ohio River. It was built Pittsburgh to Newark, and trackage rights ended just west of the Licking River at Newark.

The Columbus and Newark (thus the C&N Division) owned the railroad. It was impossible for the Panhandle to secure their own land for their railroad, so a lease agreement was drawn up. The Baltimore and Ohio owned the land, and railroad and trackage rights were granted from 1 st Street Newark to Columbus. In the later years, this was to be the finest section of railroad in the state of Ohio. The country's best passenger trains operated over the line known as the C&N Division. Coast to coast trains operated through Newark.

In the late 1 860's, after the railroad set up operation at Newark, a terminal was formed. The Sandusky Mansfield and Newark had their own St. Clair Yards, but were limited for more space. Newark Depot, or terminal headquarters, was to be built south of Main Street and on the west side of the Licking River. The main yards to be built east of the Licking River. Here was a portion of unused land about one mile wide and three miles east along the north shore of the Licking River.

The Newark Terminal had about everything needed for the transportation needs. A large classification passenger and freight yards were built. The coach yard was just west of the depot, and the machinery and freight yards, east of the river.

Fuel was to be needed to operate the many steam engines. The first engines to come to Newark were fired by wood. However, coal was more plentiful and easier to secure. Coal was mined in Perry, Muskingum, Guernsey and Belmont Counties. The railroads placed empty coal hauling cars at the mines. Thousands of cars were shipped to coal stations on the railroad.

B&O depot, Newark, Ohio, 1878.

B&O Railway shops, Newark, Ohio 1904

Water was the next thing to operate a railroad. At Newark, water for engines was secured from the Licking River. At water stations along the railroad, they took the water from creeks and streams where needed. Large water towers were built higher than the engines, hence a pumping station had to be built to pump water. Engines of small portion had to be built for the pumper stations. Scheidler Machine Works on South 1 st Street was formed to build these and other engines. These engines lasted a lifetime and beyond.

From the turn of the century the Baltimore and Ohio was the largest employer in Licking County. The economy was one of the best in the state. People came and moved to Newark to work for the B&O. From the square on Newark's east side, it was known as B&O City.

The railroads around Licking County prospered right up into the 1970's. Coal, sand, brick and cement were the main raw materials hauled into Newark Terminal.

B&O Newark Yard, 1940.

Sand was used by the glass industry, coal was used by the railroads, homes and factories for heat and usage. Brick was used for building streets and homes. Cement for concrete. Large grain elevators were constructed, slaughter houses were built, livestock pens and other factories were built. Most of these were switched and handled by railroads. Wehlre Stove Works was the nation's largest manufacturer. Heath Refinery, or Pure Oil Company, American Bottle Company all used coal from Perry County mines.

Newark Terminal, in its hey day, was one big operation. As the writer of this book, I was part of it. Thank you, B&O.

Piloted by Frank Parmelee Cincinnati to Newark

B&O PR Eastman Street, 1933. B&O's first streamlined train, piloted by Frank Parmelee, Cincinnati to Newark.

B&ORR 100 YEARS OLD NEWARK, O. 1927

Baltimore and Ohio's first engine, Newark, Ohio 1927.

First steam engine into Newark's
St. Clair Yard, 1848.

Last steam powered engine leaving
East Newark at Weiants, 1968

Straitsville Division
Information taken from time table #13

November 25, 1889
The Newark Somerset and Straitsville was organized in 1867 and built and into Shawnee
in 1871. Steel rails were laid, large cuts were carved out to grade, bridges had to be built.
The builder of the railroad made a mistake that haunted the railroad from that point on.
The cuts were too narrow for the large engines that were to come later on. Bridges were
too small for heavy weight consists, and the trestles were all wood. All of these had a
weight limit and a speed limit over them.

Coal was the number on e item on the menu for the railroad to transport. Passenger trains were to be
operated as well, and they handled everything that was used daily for the people of Perry County.
Railroads handled the mail and express.

Lets start from the Newark Terminal and head south through Licking and Perry Counties. Newark
Terminal was the main artery for Straitsville.

South Newark MP 1
After leaving Newark, crossed the Raccoon Bridge. Yes, it had a weight limit. There was industry and
stock pens and a slaughter house here.

Locust Grove MP 3.5
Crossing the Licking River Bridge, which has a weight limit, Locust Grove had an agent and passenger
station and south crossed the long trestle bridge of Hog Run Creek. Just North of Locust Grove there is a
South Fork Trestle which is all wood construction.

National Road MP 7.8
There was an agent and passenger station located north of Old Rt. 40. It had a passing siding and
livestock loading pens. This station ran competition with the Old Ohio Canal and Street Car at Hebron
Station. Also, Toledo and Ohio Central trains stopped at Hebron.

Avondale B&0 MP 10
Here Avondale borders Buckeye Lake. Had the railroad Avondale Hotel and passenger station. Avondale
Beach had swimming and boating. Also, good fishing for blue gills.

Engine 1284 at Pharis tire and rubber co.
for extra steam boilers, 1930.

B&O Roundhouse Mach., 1942

Shop men, car shops, Newark, Ohio.

B&O RR wreck crane, New. Sept. 14,1908, Newark, Ohio.

Newark depot and No. 33. Pittsburgh - Cincinnati passenger train.

5241 leads Wheeling-Chicago train 246 out of Newark, Ohio, in July of 1956.

5241 leads Wheeling-Chicago train 246 out of Newark, Ohio, in July of 1956.

Newark road engine, Newark, Ohio 1939

C&N work train, Newark, Ohio 1942

East End, North-side, Newark yard, Engineer "Joe" Beall, yard helper G. Fulck, 1947.

Newark Road engine, 1915.

Coach track depot, Newark, Ohio. #1451 Nov. 15, 1913.

The Avondale House

This was a stop point on the Straitsville Division of the B&0, known locally as the "Shawnee Dinky". Four trains with elegant, luxurious coaches attached stopped daily at the Avondale House. The hotel was a pleasure resort for fishing and hunting in the 1800's . The east end of the lake was called "True Lovers Lake".

All that remains of the pleasure resort is a set of steps that lead down the lake . Bruno was the name of the immediate area in the 1700's and 1800's . The railroad was abandoned in the 1970's and the track removed Shawnee to Interstate 70 Bridge south of National Road.

1913 B&O passenger engine, Newark, Ohio.

No 13   **Baltimore & Ohio Rail Road.**   No. 13

STRAITSVILLE DIVISION.

To take effect at 12:30 A. M., Central Standard Time, Monday, June 2, 1890, superseding Time Table No. 12, of Nov. 25, 1889.

For the government and information of Employes only, and not for the information of the public.   The Company reserves the right to vary therefrom as circumstances may require.

Straitsville timetable, 1890.

Scheidler machine works, 1905, Newark, Ohio
B&O RR switch engine.

Raccoon Creek bridge.

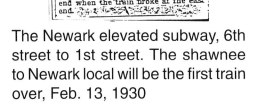

The Newark elevated subway, 6th street to 1st street. The shawnee to Newark local will be the first train over, Feb. 13, 1930

South Newark, Raccoon Creek.

South Fork of Licking River, this bridge washed out in the flood of 1913.

Dorsey Mill Road

South Fork trestle - all wood.

Locust Grove, White Chapel road.

Hog Run bridge.

"X" marks the place where engine and freight cars went in flood, this is the new bridge.

51

THE NEWARK ADVOCATE

NEWARK, OHIO, SATURDAY EVENING, MARCH 29, 1924.   ASSOCIATED PRESS COMPLETE LEASED WIRE SERVICE   VOL. 112, NO. 46.

SHAWNEE FREIGHT GOES THRU BRIDGE; FOUR MEN ARE KILLED

NEWARK TRAINMEN LOSE LIVES AT LOCUST GROVE

Trestle Collapses Under Weight of Engine Carrying Engine Crew Down With Wreckage

Four trainmen were reported killed this morning when a Shawnee local freight train crashed through a B. & O. railroad trestle over Hog Run, 5 miles southwest of Newark.

At the B. & O. offices, it was said that the engine crew went down with the wreckage.

A report to the Fitzsimmons Brothers undertaking establishment said that four persons were dead.

The B. & O. wreck crew was hurried to the scene shortly after the report of the accident was received.

The Shawnee passenger train was sent out behind the wreck train to act as a relief train.

The engine crew included Engineer E. M. Kastla, and Fireman Henry Gartner.

Brakemen on the train were Ralph Powell and John Bidwell.

The train which met with disaster was Shawnee local freight No. 184. Engine No. 2355 was in charge of Engineman Louis Kastla and Fireman H. F. Gartner.

Brakemen J. A. Bidwell and Ralph Powell were riding on the engine when the crash came.

It is believed at the Newark offices of the B. & O. railroad that the heavy rain and high water this morning undermined the bank or the abutment under the trestle which is the first bridge south of the Locut Grove station.

The bridge apparently was all right when the train approached. When the engine was fairly on the bridge it collapsed, carrying the engine into the flood waters. Eight cars followed.

At the railroad offices it was stated that the water was high enough to cover the wreckage and it is feared that if the train crew escaped death in the crash that the men were drowned while pinned under the mass of crushed timbers and twisted iron.

The freight train was the first since midnight to cross the trestle. At that time the bridge apparently was in good condition.

C. C. Larabee, conductor of the train was riding in the caboose which did not follow the other cars into the swirling waters.

There were other persons in the caboose with Larabee and all escaped.

The accident was reported as promptly as possible by Larabee and arrangements made to rush assistance to the scene of the wreck.

None of those who went down with the engine had been found at 11 o'clock.

At 11:30 o'clock it was reported to the Newark offices of the B. & O. that the waters in Hog Run were receding and that the tops of the freight cars were now visible.

Wreck, March 29, 1924

National Road depot and livestock pens.

Hotel Avondale, Buckeye Lake, Ohio.

52

Scene at Bruno, Ohio.

Thornport and Thornville After the Civil War, the Straitsville was built from Newark to Straitsville. The time was 1867, and it made its way into Shawnee in 1871. All freight at Thornport was being handled by Ohio Erie Canal boats. The canal traffic was slow, and the contents of each boat was small. The railroad breathed new life into the "Port" as freight cars and passenger trains and coal trains passed through and stopped at the "Port." This stopping and doing business brought grain elevators and hotels, and kept it a thriving trade center.

In 1884, the Columbus and Eastern, which was the Columbus Shawnee and Hocking, came and laid track throughout the southern end of "The Port." This route hauled the passengers and freight to Columbus, while the Straitsville went to Newark and Lake Erie.

Thornville was about one mile east of "The Port" and never attracted any large business. However, there were many small businesses, and it came to be a trade center.

Baltimore and Ohio took over operation of the Straitsville and put Thornport on the map. They built a large depot and freight handling building with an agent. Passenger trains stopped here for points north to Newark and south to Shawnee. Livestock pens and loading facilities were built. Team track was extended from the passing siding to furnish box cars and gondolas for shippers. Both railroads did a good business at the port until the automobile and truck came about.

More on Thornville Being a Thornville area native, I had better do a little writing on some. In the beginning, the town was called Lebanon, then New Lebanon, the Thornville in 1820. Since the first start, Thornville served a very large area as a trade center. Always small business attracted people form miles around to trade in Thornville. No large manufacturer ever located in Thornville. It did have a hotel and a bank, (my first dollar was deposited there). It also had a large town hall where all the Thornville elite met. Movies were shown here. I saw my first movie at this location in the 1930's.

There were many prominent people from the area from my start in Thornville. They had a very good school where I got my education and graduated in 1942. To this day, Thornville is more of a residential area than a business area.

Shawnee division passenger train. Avondale Buckeye Lake, Ohio, 1901.

Home of Atlee T. Wherle (Thornport), owner of Wherle Stove Co., Newark, Ohio

Columbus, Shawnee and Hocking, Rt. 13 crossing, 1910.

"Double-Header" Columbus, Shawnee and Hocking, Thornport, Ohio early 1900's.

Columbus, Shawnee and Hocking Depot, 1910, looking south from Rt. 13.

Restored U.S. Mail truck.

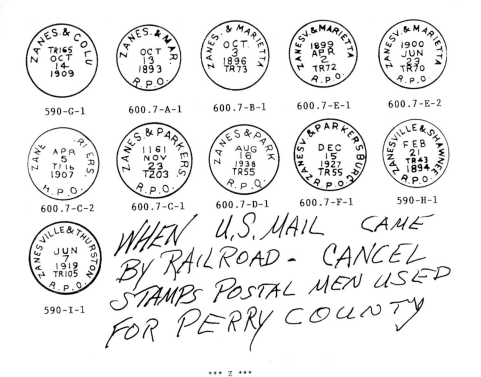

590-G-1
600.7-A-1
600.7-B-1
600.7-E-1
600.7-E-2

600.7-C-2
600.7-C-1
600.7-D-1
600.7-F-1
590-H-1

590-I-1

WHEN U.S. MAIL CAME BY RAILROAD - CANCEL STAMPS POSTAL MEN USED FOR PERRY COUNTY

Cancel stamps U.S. Postal men used for Perry County.

*** Z ***

```
Zanesville & Columbus,Oh., 67 miles, Columbus & Eastern(NYC) Ry.
    590-G-1: Zanes. & Colu(m R.P.O.), 30, black, 1909, partial, T.N., III
Zanesville & Marietta,Oh., 75 miles, Zanesville & Ohio River(B&O) R.R.
    600.7-A-1: Zanes. & Mar. R.P.O., 26.5, black, 1893, III
    600.7-B-1: Zanes. & Marietta (R.P.O.), 28, black, 1896, part, T.N., III
    600.7-E-1: Zanesv. & Marietta R.P.O., 28, black, 1899, T.N., III
    600.7-E-2: Zanesv. & Marietta R.P.O., 28.5, black, 1900,02, T.N., III
Zanesville,Oh. & Parkersburg,W.V., 88 miles, Baltimore & Ohio R.R.
    600.7-C-2: Zane(s. & Pa)r(k)ers. (R).P.O., 30, black, 1907, part, T.N., II
    600.7-C-1: Zanes. & Parkers. R.P.O., 30.5, black, 1911, T.N., II
    600.7-D-1: Zanes & Park R.P.O., 29.5, black, 1938,39,47, T.N., II
    600.7-F-1: Zanesv. & Parkersburg R.P.O., 29.5, black, 1927, T.N., II
Zanesville & Shawnee,Oh., 43 miles, Columbus,Shawnee & Hocking(NYC) Ry.
    590-H-1: Zanesville & Shawnee R.P.O., 27.5, black, 1893,94, T.N., III
Zanesville & Thurston,Oh., 39 miles, Zanesville & Western(NYC) R.R.
    590-I-1: Zanesville & Thurston R.P.O., 29.5, black, 1919, T.N., III
------------------------------------------------------------
```

Thornville school bus, 1930, courtesy of Mr. & Mrs. James White.

From Left:
Louise Courson Franks
Ruth Courson White
Lewis Courson
Bus driver is Homer Leckrone.

Thornville ladies.

Bank and Hotel, Thornville, Ohio 1930.

Town Hall, Thornville, Ohio 1900.

Public Square, Thornville, Ohio.

Columbus Street, looking East, Thornville, Ohio.

Main Street, Thornville, Ohio 1900.

B&O RR Station Master's Home, Glenford, Ohio, 1902.

B&O #208 passenger train into Glenford, 1902.

Baltimore and Ohio train, Z&W (NYC) depot station 1902, Glenford, Ohio.

Yost Station

I. Z. Shrider bought the property at Yost from Noah Leckrone in the spring of 1913. This land lies off the Frank Yost farm. The railroad made the cut off between the farms. There was a post office at Yost for a short time. One room was used for a grocery. Later a large room was built on for the general store. I. Z. Shrider was agent for the B&O ($25.00 a month). He was an express agent until about 1930. There were two passenger trains on the B&O daily. There were also the N.Y.C., local freight trains, and extra trains at times.   Farmers sent cans of cream by express to Columbus; cases of eggs and poultry were sent by express to the city. Coal was shipped on the B&O from Dixie; there were also cars of tile, fence, salt, feed, and agriculture fertilizer. Many cars of hay were loaded and sold through Hixons at Blanchester. I. Z. shipped wheat on the B&O from a building which Albert Cooperrider built about 1921. I. Z. Shrider bought the elevator (from Harry Roberts) which had been built by Bill Mechling and Albert Cooperrider. This was a big addition to the

former building. Wheat was shipped until 1925. About 1935 the Shriders moved to the farm where they lived until the death of 1. Z. Shrider in 1961, and Virge stayed there until the last few years when her health caused her to leave.   Others living in the home at Yost Station have been Leland Kaffenbergers and George Shriders. Willard Hupp owned the place for several years. A Helser family once lived there, and at the present time Mrs. Sheckley resides there.   The grain elevator is owned by Henry Frizzell and is used to store grain. It is all that remains of the once busy station at Yost Station.

Farms Up Jonathan Creek Valley
written by Carl Mechling

Farms of the Jonathan Valley are some of the most prosperous in our community. One of the main farms has been the Mechling farm west of Glenford. When Thomas Jefferson was the President of the United States and James Madison was the Secretary of State, Jacob Mechling of Pennsylvania acquired a large amount of land near Glenford, Hopewell Town ship, Perry County, Ohio, on April 3, 1808, from the U.S. Chillicothe Land Office. Jacob Mechling came to Ohio from Pennsylvania in 1816. He divided this acquired land into a farm for each of his twelve children upon his death. He gave one of these farms which is known today as the Homer Mechling farm to his youngest son, Samuel Mechling. This farm is located on State Route 204, one mile west of Glen ford. After the death of Samuel Mechling on March 12, 1849, this land was acquired by his son, Bernard Mechling, who built the large brick house in 1874. The bricks for this dwelling were made on the farm along State Route 204, on the curve by the Dorn birer farm. On February 15, 1898, the barn was remodeled, and other improvements were made to the buildings and the land. On June 26, 1964, this farm was acquired by Carl "Jim" Mechling and Harold "Hi" Mechling, sons of Homer Mechling. The farm is now owned by Carl Mechling and Shirley Mechling (Harold's daughter). Lots have been sold to Don Wilson and Patty Lewis for building new homes.

THE I. Z. SHRIDER FARM
written by Virge Shrider

In 1880 William and Emma (Cooperrider) Troup lived on the Henry Anspach farm. When their daughter, Lulu Virge, was about 10 years old (1897), they bought 50 acres of land, known as the Hughes farm, from David and Martha (Franks) Cooperrider. Bill Mechling and sons and Lewis Eis (Ice) built the barn, the house, and other buildings for them. Later William and Emma bought 20 acres more, and repair work was done on the buildings at this time. In 1903 David Cooperrider willed his daughter, Emma, land on the west and south where Poplar Fork joins Jonathan Creek (103 acres was in this farm). Emma Troup died here in 1925, and William Troup died in 1935. I. Z. and Virge (Troup) Shrider moved here after 1935. Their children, Estella, Eugene, Pauline, Woodrow, and Paul, were all born on this farm. I. Z. died in September,1961, and Virge continued to live at the farm until she was no longer able to stay alone.

Looking up Jonathan Valley

THE PAUL DEROLPH FARM
written by Paul DeRolph

This farm belonged to David Cooperrider and later to his son Murray Cooperrider. The farm house was built in 1880. When Murray Cooperrider died, his son, Wayne, took over the farm. They raised mostly beef cattle on the 300 acre farm. The next owner was Ralph Yost. Russell Palmer rented the farm from Ralph for several years. At this time the dairy farm was put in. Later Thom and Barbara (Loughman) Yost took over the farm. The farm was bought by Paul and Dorothy (Ridenour) DeRolph in 1961. They continued to run the dairy farm until 1977. Paul's son, Dennis, who lives on the back farm, helped his dad run the dairy. This back farm was purchased in 1953. At the present time Paul grain farms, raises beef cattle, and sells fertilizer, chemicals, and other farm products.

FRANK SHELLY FARM
written by Betty Shelly Loughman

The first will in our possession is that of George Shelly, Sr. It is dated October 21,1837. He gave the farm to his beloved wife, Margaret, during her life time and then it was to go to son, Michael, who was to pay a sum of money to brother Daniel. I don't know what happened to Michael. Daniel, who became the owner, was my great grandfather. Daniel's will, dated January 18, 1888, left 1/3 personal property and income to wife Catherine and the part of the house she occupied; to her during her lifetime. (She could also keep two cows). Jefferson, my grandfather, was to inherit the entire farm at the death of Catherine, providing he pay the sum of $2,500.00 to his sister Elve Ann, wife of Amos Albert. Jefferson had the following children: Emmett, Dennis, Harvey, Nettie, George, Frank, and Anna. My father paid off each of the heirs one at a time. The house was built when he was 5 years old. He was born in 1880. Frank Shelly died in 1964. He left the farm to Willard, Lucille, Emogene, and Betty. A plot of land was donated to the Glenford community for a park, known as Shelly Park.

THE FRED MECHLING FARM
written by Helen Hursey

The Peter P. Mechling farm, known as "Meadow Stock Farm", is a part of the land which Peter's father, Samuel Mechling, inherited from his father, Jacob Mechling, in April, 1831. Peter P. Mechling purchased the land in two tracts. On June 27, 1868, he was deeded 109 acres of land from Magdelena (Poorman) Mechling and Bernard Mechling (wife and son of Samuel). This land was the south part of the northwest quarter of Section No. 8, Township No. 17, and Range 16. On March 31, 1883, Peter P. Mechling purchased the second tract containing 40 acres from Bernard Mechling and Leah (Zartman) Mechling, his wife. This was part of the north half of the above section. These two tracts made a total of 149 acres which included the Jonathan Creek and two railroads, Columbus and Eastern, later called the Baltimore and Ohio (B. & O.), and the Zanesville and Western (Z & W). After Peter P. Mechling's death on April 22, 1922, Fred Mechling, his son, purchased the farm from Peter's heirs, H. Orval Mechling, Bertha (Mechling) Walser, and Frank D. Mechling on June 21, 1922. Upon the death of Fred S. Mechling, January 17, 1965, Bessie (Parks) Mechling sold the farm to her daughter, Helen, and her husband, Donnard Hursey. After the death of Donnard Hursey on March 7, 1970, the farm was transferred to Helen Hursey, the present owner.

RALPH COOPERRIDER FARM
written by Ralph Cooperrider

This farm is located west of Glenford up the Jona than Valley. It belonged to Rezin Franks in 1883. The next owner was David and Martha (Franks) Cooper rider in 1893. It was left to his son, Frank Cooperrider, in 1899. His wife was Edith (Daugherty). At the present time Ralph Cooperrider (Frank's son) owns the farm. He and his wife, Esta (Orr), purchased the farm in 1920 and moved there in 1947. He has raised grain and livestock on his farm.

HENRY FRIZZELL FARM
written by Henry Frizzell

The former Frank Yost farm, located up Jonathan Valley, has been a grain farm for many years. Frank's son, Ralph, built the metal building in 1938 for selling seed grain which was raised on the farm. At one time he employed eight men to help with the raising and selling of the seed corn. The beautiful brick home is over 200 years old. In 1957 Henry and Jettie Frizzell bought the land from Ralph Yost. At the present time Mr. Frizzell owns 170 acres of land. For sometime he did some seed cleaning for the farmers around the area. He also raises grain and livestock. His son, Joe, lives on the farm south of this farm. He does bulldozing and excavating.

WAL-MEC FARM
written by Paul Mechling

Wal-Mec Farm was purchased by the present owners, Paul Parks and Annabell (Wallace) Mechling, on February 13,1968, from the estate of William H. Walser. W. H. Walser and his wife, Bertha (Mechling) Walser, had purchased most of the farm from her parents, Peter and Frances Mechling, grandparents of Paul Mechling. Records show that the land was transferred in three different tracts. These 183 acres were obtained in 1895 by Peter P. Mechling and his wife from James and Patsey Egan, heirs of Patrick Egan, who had purchased the land from the estate of John Stockberger in 1855. Earlier owners were Peter Dumbelt (1827) and Elizabeth McInturf (1823). In 1913 W. H. Walser purchased 33 acres from Charles O'Bannon. This land was adjacent to the 50 acres purchased earlier and extended north to the county line road. Previous owners of these acres include Olive Foster, Robert Yost, Abe Lewis, and Moses Granger. In 1973-76 the present owners remodeled, restored, and added to the brick house located on the tract of land south of State Route 204. They moved into the modernized home in the sum mer of 1976. The 206 acres continue to be operated as a grain, hay, and beef cattle farm.

Glenford Mill

One of the first industries of Glenford was the mills that lined the banks of Jonathan Creek. One of the largest grist mills, built about 1820, was owned and operated by Peter King. The next owners were Levi and Austin Cooperrider, who operated it until after 1910. The last operator was John Love. The old mill burned in June 1913. A sawmill owned and operated by "Sawmill Pete" Mechling was just north of Glen ford. (Pete Mechling was the father of Fenton Mechling). Another mill was in this area, but there is no information on it. The Rousculp Mill was east of Glenford.

Grist Mill, destroyed by fire in 1913

B&O Railroad Depot - NYC Railroad Depot

Railroads

With the coming of the railroads around 1871 Glenford began to prosper. The B&O and the N.Y. Central were the main companies. George Andrews was a section foreman and was followed by Charlie Starkey, who held the job for over thirty-seven years. At one time there were eight passenger trains and several freight trains (hauling coal and cattle). The "High Ball Express" ran through Glentord regularly. There was a N&W Stockyard back of the depot. Weigh scales were south of the post office building (North Main Street). In the 1900's Fred Soliday became the station master and telegraph operator. The next operator was Pansy Clark, and the last operator was Olive (Ridenour) Danison. The old B&O red station house was torn down sometime in the early 1930's, the Z&W freight office and telegraph office in 1944, and the old water tower in 1959. In 1976 the tracks were removed, the last reminder of the busy railroad station of Glenford.

New Quarry.

1974-76, new tramway coming into plant at Glassrock.

Factories

The Glentord Manufacturing Company were dealers in lumber and coal. They manufactured crates, boxes, flooring, and siding. They also operated a planing mill. The company was established February 24, 1904. The following businessmen were officers and managers: George Ice, President; D. H. King, Treasurer; W. S. Johnston, Vice-President; and George Swinehart, Secretary and Manager. They maintained a modern well equipped plant, gave steady employment to twenty men, and enjoyed a large trade in the community. A fence factory was located near the railroad tracks back of the Hazlett grocery store on South Main Street. It was operated by Herb and George Carnicom and was converted to a grist mill. A title plant owned and operated by Ben Leckrone and Harvey Shelly was later sold to Charles Smith and then torn down. A tile plant was owned and operated by Charles Swinehart just east of Glenford at one time. Raymond Denison operated a cement block factory on East High Street. Reno Swinehart was his helper. Fred Soliday operated a cement warehouse near the railroad tracks north of High Street. E. P. Reed was stock and wool buyer for several years in this community. Carl Johnston and Joe Hatfield had an ice house not far from the depot. Irvin Cooperrider and Perry Orr had an ice house near Perry's home on South Main Street.

Lumbering

One of the first dealers in lumber and lumber products was Oscar Ridenour. Starting in the 1930's and until his death in 1976, he was active in the business. At the present time Cecil Snider is in the logging business and is a timber buyer. He and his wife Maxine are also involved in stock car racing. Joe King and his sons have a sawmill and make pallets. Robert Daugherty, whose business is known as the D&P Speciality Company, started in 1972 and at this time handles only wood products. Roy Launder is a timber and wood buyer.

Oscar J. Ridenour, Lumber King.

Arrow points in box factory back of B&O depot.

Grocery Stores

The first stores were the huckster wagons, which served the country for many years. They were operated by Wallace King, Cass Hazlett, LeRoy Gordon, and Guy and Emmett Shrider. The first grocery store was the S. R. Johnston Store on Mill Street, followed by the W. R. Hazlett store on the corner of High and South Main Street. Hazlett later sold to Percy Smith. Wallace King had a grocery at one time in Glenford. The first owners of the grocery on North Main Street were Bernard Mechling and W. V. Zartman. The next owner was J. D. Findlay (who came from Johnstown, Pa., in 1894). He and his partner, N. W. Roberts, carried on the business for 13 years. The next owner was E. M. Shangle. E. L. Shrider bought the store from him in 1925 and operated it until 1945. He sold to Willard Shelly who sold to Dr. Pope, and in the early 1950's Pope sold to Morton and Lucille (Shelly) Hamilton. The store was operated for a while by Kenneth and Emagene (Shelly) Shelton. Then it was purchased by Luke and Bernice (Watkins) Swinehart in 1956. At this time Steve and Lou Swinehart are the owners of the only store in Glenford.

E.L. Shrider Grocery Store, Carl H. Johnston.

Luke and Bernice Swinehart, Grocery Store.

E.L., G.V., and I.Z. Shrider, grocery operators and sister Josie.

Steve and Estilina Swinehart, Country Mart - Steve and Luke.

Post Office

The first post office was in the Seth E. Johnston store (south of Glenford). Mail was brought from Somerset, and people picked up their mail at the store. Official date for the first Glenford Post Office was May 3, 1871, and S. R. Johnston was postmaster. The post office was moved to the depot building and later to many other buildings in Glenford. Post masters were Mollie Johnston, Melancton Mechling, Alonze Legge, William Johnston, Laura Lentz, and Melancton "Doc" Zartman. A post office was built in~ 1910-11 on North Main Street. In 1914 Fenton Mechling became postmaster. He and his wife, Annabelle, had a small grocery beside the post office. His wife, Annabelle, became postmaster after his death and held this position until 1949. At this time Willard Shrider was appointed temporary post master and served until Gerald Danison was appointed in 1951. Olive (Ridenour) Danison was assistant at this time. She was appointed postmaster in 1954 and is the present postmaster. Her assist ants have been Ina Kelly, Doris Lattimer, and Bessie Swinehart. Mail carriers have been Frank Ridenour, Arthur Starkey, William Kelly, Homer Smith, Carl Johnston, Oscar Leckrone, Gerald Danison, and, at the present time, Nolan Henderson. Some assistant mail carriers have been Urban Foucht, Clyde Noyes, Karl Kaffenberger, Myron Ridenour, Gomer Roberts, Tom Yost, Bob Daugherty, Byron Kaffenberger, Richard Ridenour, and, at the present time, Jim Poorman.

First Post Office in Glenford, 1871.

Old Post Office , Confectionery, and Hotel.

Glenford Post Office

CHALFANT STATION

The little town of Chalfant named for Robert Chalfant is located about two miles southeast of Glen ford. Since a depot was there, it was generally known as Chalfant Station. During the horse and buggy and wagon era, Chalfant was a very busy and enterprising place. It boasted a butcher shop, a carpenter shop, a blacksmith shop, a school house, and a general store which not only sold merchandise but included a post office as well. Mr. Paine was the first blacksmith. When he retired, the shop was operated by Dave Kinder. Soon after, it was closed due to the lack of business. Albert Chalfant was the first store keeper and butcher. After his death David Leckrone operated the store, post office, and depot. Along with the operating of the above, he bought hay and wheat which was shipped on the B&O railroad. The railroad did a flourishing business at that time. They maintained a stockyard and ramp, where livestock was loaded on the cars. Ship timber, sawed logs, railroad ties, and all kinds of lumber were loaded here. Due to illness Mr. Leckrone had to close the store. It burned to the ground soon after. The store was the real landmark where the old timers met and swapped tales. With the coming of the R.F.D. the post office along with the other businesses closed. With consolidation of schools the children were bussed to other schools, and Chalfant School was closed. Chalfant is now a quiet, well-kept little community.

Chalfant's Station.

Mabel Gunion Coble at Chalfant Station
(arrow points to store in background).

GLASS ROCK

The land around Glass Rock was owned by one Denison. Plans were to call it "Station Hilda" for his wife. Since there was a great amount of rock in the area, it was decided to call it Glass Rock. This was about 90 years ago. The railroad at that time was the C.S.&H. (Columbus, Shawnee, Hocking). At that time there were two round trips, passenger trains, a local freight, and a through freight. In order to take care of all the trains there were a water tank, a section house, and passing tracks that held seventy cars. The store was built by Wallace King. Then a Mr. Wilson ran the store. The next owner was G. W. Gordon. After a number of years he sold the store to Noah Swinehart (his son-in-law). After operating the store for several years, he rented the store to Charlie Ridenour, who ran a creamery along with the store. In 1915 the store was sold to E. L. Shrider, who owned it from 1915-1919. G. V. Shrider purchased the store from his brother. G. V. Shrider operated the elevator, the railroad office, and the store from 1919 1941 . In the meantime he purchased 3/4 acres from Willis Cooperrider and built a storage building across the street. Raymond Curry bought a lot next to it and built a garage. It is now owned by the Dale Garey family, dealers in Allis Chalmers farm equipment. In the summer of 1941 the store was sold to A. B. Swinehart. This year, 1978, Nancy James and Jane Gordon purchased the store. Clair Bowser owned two lots—the one which the Shriders bought and where they now live, the other purchased and built on by Ray Sturgeon and now owned by Roberta Garrett. In 1948 Mr. Shrider sold the elevator to the Farm Bureau and continued to work for the N.Y. Central railroad. N.Y. Central built a small office across the track. Mr. Shrider worked for them for over 40 years. The new Central Silica tramway crosses over Glass Rock. Another business place in Glass Rock besides the one mentioned is the trucking business of Tom Trailer. This business was formerly owned and operated by Paul Coble, whose son, Jim, drove for him. Ruth (Curry) Shrider and daughter Polly and Judy (Sturgeon) Bowser and husband Mike are the other residents. Mr. Shrider was always active in the community and enjoyed his farm. This was written by Mr. Shrider before his death February 5, 1978.

Mr. and Mrs. George Gordon, 1910, at Glassrock.

Glassrock Store.

Glenford water station, used by both B&O RR and Z&W RR, 1902.

Walser's Curve

The Columbus and Eastern (CH&S) Crossing. A target controlled the B&O and C&E movement. There was no person to control the target. Vertical position for C&E position. This meant that the B&O had to stop, and after seeing no train approaching, threw target and moved over. Rear end trainman restored target to C&E. Also passenger stop signal.

Yost Station MP 13

The Shrider family had a grain elevator and a railroad spur.

Glenford MP 17.8

Glenford was some station. The station master's home was located just north of water tower, and he kept the water bin full of£ water. The C&E and B&O both took on water here.

There was a passenger and freight depot agent which did a great amount of business. A passing siding, a transfer track with the C&E, and a team track. The transfer track was used for and movement from Glass Rock to Newark Glass Makers. The C&E had a depot agent operator. There, trains ran from Zanesville, Fultonham to Thurston.

Chalfants MP 19.8

Passing siding and passenger depot, which was no more than a shed.

Belden Brick Plant MP 23

Makers of building brick. Shipped many car loads everywhere.

Lee's Siding MP 23.8

Just a passing siding. Coal trains had to double here because of Somerset grade. Also a passenger station stop on signal.

Somerset MP 24.4

Agent operator controlled Somerset area. It was a brick depot for passengers and Express and U.S. Mail. Team track along side of depot. Lumber and planning mill loading. Somerset Cut was cut out of solid rock. It was narrow and straight cut. In the winter time water would freeze and make large icicles, which would hit the rail cars when movement was made through. At South Somerset there was a team track and an elevator which did grain business.

Somerset Trestle MP 25

This trestle was some wood working making this bridge. It was all wood, and around 800 feet long and 70 feet high in the middle. Yes, it vibrated a little when two engine and a coal train moved over it. It was built on the Somerset Grade.

B&O and Z&W Depot, Glenford, Ohio.

B&O RR, Somerset, Ohio depot, 1898

B&O RR, Somerset depot, Straitsville, division, 1905.

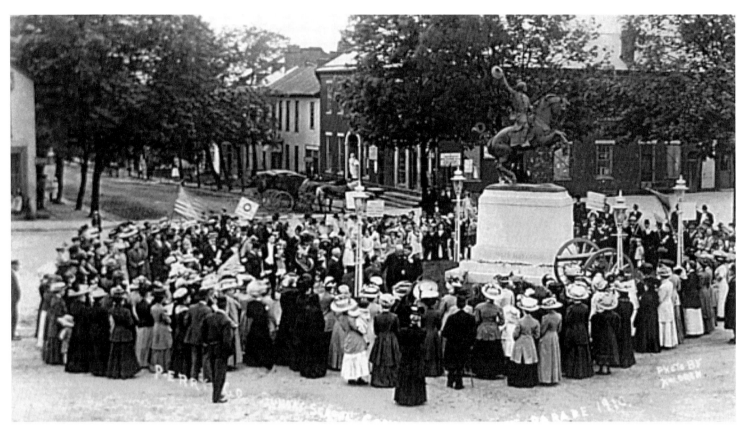

Perry County Sunday school convention, honoring General Phil Sheridan, 1910.

B&O cut looking North, Somerset, Ohio, 1905.

Somerset Trestle.

By 1883, the town had a population of about 500 people. It contained a post office, C&MV RRd, TB & CO RRd, Gardner agent, B&O RRd, Barke agent, Larimer's Sheridan House, and another hotel, Stolzenbach merchandise as well as Gordon and Bringardner merchandise, Rarick Boot and Shoemaker, Ryan druggist and pharmacy, Bringardner Hardware, Clark ad Flowers druggists, furniture and livery, Edmiston bar and billiards, a flouring mill, newspaper, tow millinery stores, four physicians, and meat shop. John Bringarnder, Son Al Bringardner, and son-in-law, B.F. Conkle were co-owners of the bentworks. The brick tow story school building on Hill Street was administered by Prof. John Crosbie.

The town was incorporated between 1883 and 1885. About this time, "Whiskey Row" was doing its best business. The row also called the Potomac, was a group of saloons across the tracks facing the village. They extended the length of seven or more saloons. The first saloon was built by a Dr. Clark who started to build it in the morning and by night had a keg of beer behind the counter. The sign above the door was Do Drop Inn. These were all erected on a board platform which held the buildings high and dry, in those days water often stood there.

There was a large two storied building, the Union Depot. Large flocks of turkeys and chickens were shipped to eastern markets as well as tobacco brought from south of town, along with blackberries, and apples from one of the oldest and best orchards, planted by Johnny Appleseed. Piles of split wood were brought in and thrown off wagons for firewood. Mrany fires were common, some caught from the railroad.

Above one saloon was a barber shop run by a rather unusual person...a colored man. He was the only Negro ever known to live in Junction City. He was well thought of, but a man named Short taunted him one day, and with a quick move, the Negro flashed a razor, hurled it at Short. It reached its mark, 11 times until his target was mutilated. A large crowd gathered, consensus was to hang the barber from the big sycamore tree by Rush Creek. This was averted by High Murphy, constable. They hurried him away to jail in New Lexington, where he stood trial and was sent to prison. Short recovered.

Junction City, Ohio State Prison.

Perry County Oil Boom, Junction City, Ohio.

Wellan's MP 27.1
At the foot of Somerset Grade. A passing siding was located here, and it was a passenger stop.

Gobles MP 21
Water station only.

Junction City Ohio State Prison This prison is located west of Junction City and North of Rt. 37 about one mile. It housed many prisoners of various crimes. They had their own farm and gardens, and they raised their own food supply. The farm was beautifully kept and maintained by the prisoners. They had a railroad spur because they made paving and building brick for the state, and it was shipped by rail all over the state.

I now want to tell a true story about the Warden's chair. It was the Spring of 1945. It seems that the Warden broke his chair, or else it just wore out, so he ordered two to be shipped by the B&O Railroad. I was the head brakeman on the Local on the day the chairs arrived. We had his chairs on the Way car. Normally, the Junction City freight would be left at the freight house, but he needed the chairs, so the Agent Somerset asked us to deliver his chairs at the main prison gate. Upon arrival at the gate, Conductor Carlyle and I opened the Way car door, and the guard (with a shotgun), brought two prisoners out to the train. Each one took a chair and reentered the prison. The chairs must have fit the Warden's torso, because he waved to us as the train went by his home on our way to Shawnee.

Junction City MP 33.2
Agent operator, passenger station depot, passing siding and a transfer track with C&MV Railroad. Transferred brick and tile from Rush Creek Brick. Hank thrown target with C&MV. This type of target was one of a kind. It was no more than a crank turn screw, ~d ~t was slow at that. Target was operated by train crew. C&MV was vertical - Horizontal B&O to be left C&MV.

Bristol MP 38
Here starts the Perry county coal fields. Just north of north portal of tunnel is Bristol siding, which is stub ended. This siding was mostly used for coal trains doubling Bristol Hill. Bristol Tunnel was around 800 feet long, and built on a curve and under Bristol Hill. South of the tunnel on the right is Bristol Block Mine. Loaded out around 10 cars a day.

Dickson MP 30.6
This was a passenger station stop, and the big Dixie Mine was located here. Dixie operated around the clock, which required Shawnee Yard engine to switch.

McCuneville Kehota Mine was located here. It was some operation. They had their own engine and cars to pull coal from the pit to the screening tipple. There were tracks here to hold many Coal cars. There was a coal station here. Shawnee area engines coaled here.

Rock Run Branch MP 42.5

Rock Run Branch ran from the junction to Old Straitsville. On this branch was located B&O Mine #3, Shawnee Flash Brick Sidewell Mine. Around 30 carloads of coal, and three cars of brick came off this branch each day. Shawnee Flash Brick made paving brick, and many brick loads came from here. From the B&O's mine came all company fuel. Later, this branch was used by strip mined loading.

Shawnee MP 43.7

After leaving Rock Run Switch, the water station was located just north of Wye switch. Here is where engines cleaned their fire and took on water. Wye track was used to turn engines, and on the tail end of Wye, about one mile, was the Whippoorwill Mine. There were three tracks into it. They loaded out around 20 cars each day. Then came Shawnee storage tracks. Here is where Mty box cars and coal hoppers were stored.

House track at the depot for inbound freight for local use. The depot housed an agent and an operator, and was used for passengers, U.S. Mail Express, and coal mine workers waiting on trains. The yard engine was kept close by.

Ohio Mineral and Mining Clay Craft This was located about one and one half miles from the depot. They had two plants. They mined their own clay and made two types of brick. One was road paving and the other was building brick. This plant was joint switched by the CH&S Columbus Hocking and Straitsville. Then was called Zanesville and Western.

At the transfer track, cars were interchanged with B&O. The Zanesville and Western (CH&S) had a depot on the corner of Straitsville Road that ran through Hemlock and all stations over the Corning. Coal miners used this train to San Toy Mines over at Sayre.

New Straitsville The Hocking Valley Railroad came into Straitsville from the southwest direct from their main of Hocking Valley from Columbus. They had a mine on the South Rock Run Branch, but never interchanged with the B&O. Hocking Valley did a lot of freight business other than coal. They had a passenger train from Straitsville over to their main. It was a combination car on a freight train, doubled as a caboose.

Robinson's Cave New Straitsville Birth place of United Mine Workers of America. The entrance to Robinson's Cave has a carousel that provided entertainment for Straitsville families. Here, Chris Evans and disillusioned miners met in secret to organize the UMW in 1890. He later became national secretary of that Union.

There were many blood-shed fights among the miners and company-hired thugs before the Unions finally organized most of the mines.

North Portal, Bristol Tunnel.

B&O Conductor Frank Crist in front of South
portal of the Bristol Tunnel, 1952.

One tunnel on Straitsville, Bristol South portal.

Bristol Block Mine Perry County, 1905.

Columbus Shawnee & Hocking

The railroad was built out of Columbus in 1883. The first timecard I could find was November 1894. It was built around High Street Yards because it came out to Alum Creek Junction. There it connected to the T&OC, then it ran on T&OC to Thurston. There it branches off, then through Thornport. After arrival at Thornport, it opened transportation freight and people travel on trains. Crossed the B&O at Walser's (B&O crossing on their time card) Yost station, then Glenford. Here they had a telegraph station, depot for freight and passengers. Interchanged cars with B&O, which also had the same facilities. Then Glass Rock, here was a sand procession plant that supplied sand for glass making at Lancaster Newark and Columbus that all went by rail. Through Mt. Perry to Fultonham over to Sayre. The on the T&OC to Corning Terminal. CS&H left Corning west by the Congo Mine, then Drakes, Buckingham, Hemlock, had a telegraph station and agent. Carrington was next, then Mine 21. Shawnee Station was next. This is as far as the CS&H ran. They had planned in early stages to build to Straitsville, but the NS&S built it from Rock Run southeast to Straitsville.

CS&H at Shawnee built a passenger depot which was one of a kind. The west side was round with all glass windows. In early 1900 this railroad was purchased by Zanesville and western, hence Z&W. This is where it got its nickname "Zig Zag and Wobble." There was a small rail yard built to handle local freight and transfer with B&O. Joint switched the Ohio Mineral and Mining (Clay Craft) with B&O.

Ran passenger trains daily. Shawnee east to Corning, and all points on the Z&W T&OC and K&M. T&OC ran from Toledo through Columbus to Corning. Then the K&M, which was the Kanawha and Michigan. It ran to Charleston, West Virginia. At Corning Terminal there was a large freight yard and passenger terminal. Here was a crew change and round house for servicing the many engines. Here was where freight trains were built for points north and south.

Here at Corning Roundhouse, when drilling for the first deep water well, they struck oil and set off the Perry County oil boom, which extended west to Bremen and Fairfield County. Coal and oil were the main products that the railroads transported.

All of these roads were joined together with New York Central.

At New Lexington they jointed with Cincinnati and Muskingum Valley C&MV, which ran from Trinway through Zanesville to Lebanon, then to Cincinnati. This line was later taken over by PRR Pennsy.

So the Central and PRR both used the line New Lexington to Bremen. It was owned by C&MV or PRR, Central had trackage right to the end, then Penn Central. The NYC abandoned the Shawnee in the early 1940's, and the B&O did the same in 1973, ending rail service that had lasted over 100 years.

Creeley Mine, Peabody Coal Company, Shawnee, Ohio, 1900.

Kehota Mining Co., McCuneville, Ohio.

Kehota Mining Co., McCuneville, Ohio, Shawnee District.

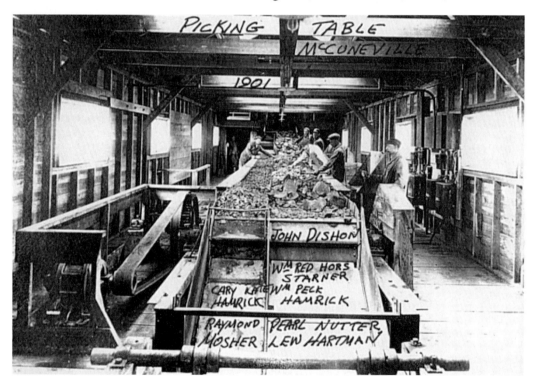

Kehota Mine, picking table, McCuneville, Ohio, 1901.

People in photo are:
John Dishon
William Red Horse Starner
Cary Kate Hamrick
William Peck Hamrick
Raymond Mosher
Pearl Nutter
Lew Hartman

I was a member (Head Brakeman) of the crew that brought the last train out of Shawnee area. Pictures taken of the train by the newspaper. Clay Craft gave each member of the crew two bricks. I still have mine to remind me of the Perry County railroads and products that came from there.

After the Shawnee shut down, all employees that worked for the B&O transferred to Newark. In the hey day of Perry County railroading, were many Perry County people who worked for the PRR - NYC and B&O, I myself being one of them.

Engine 2357 on Shawnee Local, 1938.

Shawnee yard engine, Jim Shea and Crew, 1901.

Being a member of this train crew (Head Brakeman), this is how it was done. All persons that manned the train are true. There were two engines. First Engineer was Louis Wainwright, and his Fireman was Ralph Fairall. Second engine was C. "Peg" Clary, and his Fireman was Nell Goff. Engineer Clary had a wooden leg from the knee down. He lost his leg in a rail accident.

The Conductor was George Pleat, a former Shawnee Yard Conductor. The Flagman was H.C. "Red" Burns, and he came from the Shawnee area. The Head Brakeman was "CT" Winegardner from the Thornville area.

We were called for 9:00pm. The train consist were two engines, 40 Mty Mine Hoppers and a 1434 caboose. Arriving for duty, the engine crew after 9:00pm got their engines fired up and watered. The train crew reported to the Yard Master Heffely. Scrap was his nickname. The Yard Master informed us that the train was made up and ready for engines.

After getting both engines coupled together, were placed on train and air hoses coupled and train was turned over to car inspectors for the air test. Conductor Pleart secured the train orders and messages and delivered them to train crew. Air test complete, the train was ready to proceed to the Perry County Coal Fields, which is 43 miles due south.

The speed limit on the Shawnee was 25mph, except over wooden bridges and trestles. There it was IO m.p.h.. Leaving Newark Yard, crossed the Licking River, Raccoon Creek, then at River, crossed south fork of Licking River. South of Locust Grove, crossed Dutch Fork called Hog Run. At this bridge a great disaster happened in 1924.

Then came National Road (U.S. 40) Harbor Hills, then Avondale. Around Buckeye Lake we came to Edgewater. Thornport was next, crossed Route 13 here, then ran parallel with the NYC to Walser. Here the train was stopped for the Head Brakeman had to throw target for B~O. After train pulled over crossing, Flagman restored target. Then came Yost Station, Shrider's Elevator, then Jonathon Creek. Here was where water was pumped to supply the water tower at Glenford. The water tower sat between both railroads and was used by both for the engines. Glenford was a great town. There was Swinehart's Country Store, an transfer track to service both railroads, a long passing siding.

Leaving Glenford, we passed Chalfants, then came Belden Brick, then Lee's. Somerset was next, turn of century depot a house track and agent operator, daylight hours only. Then Somerset cut under Route 13, then South Somerset, Logan Road had to be protected of highway traffic. Leaving Somerset next was the large wooden trestle. This was some tresle, as it was all wood. When two engines and a coal train pulled over it, it vibrated and you could see the ripples in the water below.

B&O Railroad depot, Shawnee, Circa 1900.

Whippoorwill Mine, #3211, Shawnee, Ohio. (On end of Wye, last name Giblow).

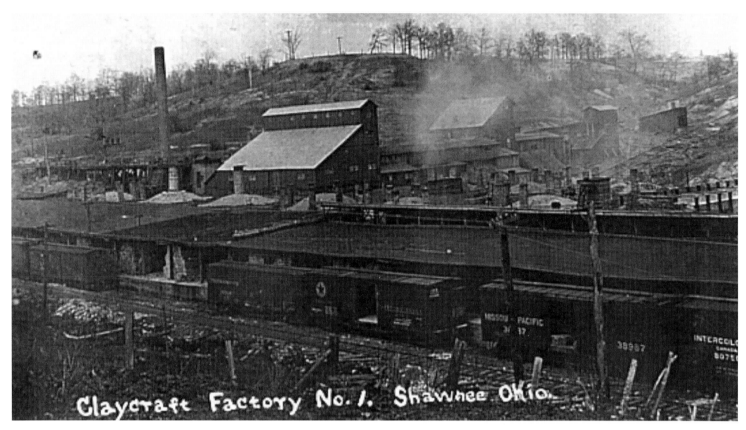

Ohio mineral and mining, Claycraft, Shawnee, Ohio.

Rock Run, B&O owned Mine No. 3.

Sidwell Mine, Rock Run.

Flash Brick, Rock Run, Shawnee, Ohio.

Then came Wellan, then Gobles. Here was a water station. Then the State Prison Junction City. Railroad serviced this plant. They made brick for state use. Now we crossed Route 37 in Junction City. A target, "one of a kind" to throw. You didn't throw it, you turned a crank screw. This was the Head Brakeman's job. After train proceeded over, the Flagman restored it. Crossed the Pennsy and NYC here. Leaving Junction City, we came to Bristol Siding, then Bristol Tunnel.

Now we enter the coal mines. Placed five MTY. In Pike Mine. We have 10 Hops for Bristol, which have to be dropped in. The local had picked up Bristol Coal and taken to Newark.

Leaving Bristol we crossed Dixie Road, then came McCuneville. Route 75 traffic had to be protected. Now we arrived at Rock Run Junction and the real work begins. Have 20 Hops for here, 10 for Cincinnati and 10 for Sidwell

Train was stopped back just east of McCuneville crossing. Engines were cut off and proceeded into Rock Run. Set the coal out to and down the main. Flagman bled all air brakes on train, and entire train was dropped into Rock Run. Sidwell and Cincinnati Mine pulled and placed with emptys. Coal was picked up and placed against the caboose, was shoved to Wye track Shawnee.

We had the five Mtys for Giblow next to engines. Giblow Mine was on the tail end of Wye track. After pulling five loads and placing five Myts, turned engines and coal coming off Wye.

Here at Shawnee, the Conductor registered in at the agent depot and secured any agent's orders. Both engines fires were cleaned and watered. Picked up 15 loads of coal from siding, which meant we were to have 40 loads of coal for Newark.

At McCuneville, both engines were filled to the limit with coal. Next came doubling the Bristol Hill. Twenty cars were taken to and backed in at Bristol Siding. Train was doubled and ready to proceed to Junction City at Clark's Restaurant for breakfast.

After eating, the train crossed the Pennsy and NYC north. Stopped at Gobles and both engines watered. Then came doubling Somerset Hill to Lee's siding. Twenty cars first cut, then 20 and caboose next. Operator at Somerset was on duty and a meet order with the local was for National Road.

Leaving Somerset area, we started for Glenford. Did not stop for water. Would have enough to get to Newark. Crossed Walser, then through Thornport. Next came Avondale Grade. Started to pick up speed for the run over to Harbor Hills. Over the grade, we could see National Road. The Local was there in the siding as we passed.

Hocking Valley Rail Road, New Straitsville, Ohio.

Home of the founding United Mine Workers of America, 1890 - Chris Evans, organizer.

Cincinnati, Wilmington, and Zanesville
AIR LINE
RAILROAD!

This Road is 132½ miles in length, passing through the county seats of Muskingum, Perry, Fairfield, Pickaway, Fayette and Clinton counties. Connects at Morrow with the Little Miami Railroad, for all points South and West; and at Zanesville with the Central Ohio Railroad, for all points East.

MAIL LINE COACHES leave Lancaster DAILY, for Logan and Athens; and Circleville, for Chillicothe and Portsmouth.

THROUGH TICKETS EASTWARD, for sale at Little Miami Depot, Cincinnati, and THROUGH TICKETS WESTWARD, for sale at Office corner Second and Main streets, Zanesville.

WM. KEY BOND, Receiver,   **B. D. ABBOTT, Asst. Sup't,**
Cincinnati.   Zanesville.

JOS. J. GEST, General Ticket Agent, Cincinnati.

STATIONS.

Miles.		Miles.		Miles.
0	Zanesville,	168	77 Four Corners,	90
½	Putnam,	167½	81 New Holland,	87
10	Rossville,	157	90 WASHINGTON,	77
15	McLuney,	152	95 Jasper,	72
21	NEW LEXINGTON,	146	101 Sabina,	66
26	Wolfs,	141	104 Reesville,	64
33	Bremen,	134	107 Wilsons,	60
37	Berne,	130	112 WILMINGTON,	55
42	LANCASTER,	125	117 Linden,	50
52	Amanda,	115	121 Clarksville,	46
57	Stouts,	110	127 Hicks,	41
64	CIRCLEVILLE,	103	132 MORROW,	36
70	Yellow Bird,	97	168 Cincinnati,	0
75	Williamsport,	92		

Cincinnati, Wilmington and Zanesville Railroad time tables.

When railroads handled the U.S. Mail. Cancel stamps postal employees used on the trains listed below.

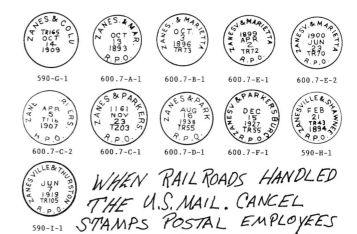

WHEN RAILROADS HANDLED THE U.S. MAIL. CANCEL STAMPS POSTAL EMPLOYEES USED ON TRAINS BELOW

```
                                   *** Z ***

Zanesville & Columbus,Oh., 67 miles, Columbus & Eastern(NYC) Ry.
    590-G-1: Zanes. & Colu(m R.P.O.), 30, black, 1909, partial, T.N., III
Zanesville & Marietta,Oh., 75 miles, Zanesville & Ohio River(B&O) R.R.
    600.7-A-1: Zanes. & Mar. R.P.O., 26.5, black, 1893, III
    600.7-B-1: Zanes. & Marietta (R.P.O.), 28, black, 1896, part, T.N., III
    600.7-E-1: Zanesv. & Marietta R.P.O., 28, black, 1899, T.N., III
    600.7-E-2: Zanesv. & Marietta R.P'.O., 28.5, black, 1900,02, T.N., III
Zanesville,Oh. & Parkersburg,W.V., 88 miles, Baltimore & Ohio R.R.
    600.7-C-2: Zane(s. & Pa)r(k)ers. (R).P.O., 30, black, 1907, part, T.N., II
    600.7-C-1: Zanes. & Parkers. R.P.O., 30.5, black, 1911, T.N., II
    600.7-D-1: Zanes & Park R.P.O., 29.5, black, 1938,39,47, T.N., II
    600.7-F-1: Zanesv. & Parkersburg R.P.O., 29.5, black, 1927, T.N., II
Zanesville & Shawnee,Oh., 43 miles, Columbus,Shawnee & Hocking(NYC) Ry.
    590-H-1: Zanesville & Shawnee R.P.O., 27.5, black, 1893,94, T.N., III
Zanesville & Thurston,Oh., 39 miles, Zanesville & Western(NYC) R.R.
    590-I-1: Zanesville & Thurston R.P.O., 29.5, black, 1919, T.N., III
*****************************************************************************
```

Hemlock Depot, 1903.

This was Hemlocks first depot, it was torn down around 1909, and another built on west side of Main Street. This depot was located on the east side of Main Street. The two men in the photo are L-R - Chas. Kunce and Pierce Osenbaugh.

Zanesville & Western RAILWAY.

2 TRAINS DAILY WITH THROUGH COACHES

.... BETWEEN ...

ZANESVILLE & COLUMBUS
CROOKSVILLE & COLUMBUS
SHAWNEE & COLUMBUS
ZANESVILLE & SHAWNEE
ZANESVILLE & CORNING
ZANESVILLE & RENDVILLE
ZANESVILLE & CROOKSVILLE

Direct Connection at Columbus and Zanesville for all points.

Excursions every Sunday to Columbus Zanesville at Low Rates.

Below in picture is track crew on Z.+W. around Hemlock, Standing L-R Ed Dunlap; John Thornton, Seated L-R Harl Secrest, Jim Jenks.

1903

Time Table 1916, Shawnee Jct. on B&O, Z&OR over to San Toy.

WESTWARD.

	Train Order Stations.	New England Sub-Division. TIME-TABLE No. 29. May 28, 1916.	Passing Siding Capacity in Cars.	59 FRIDAY ONLY P. M.	SECOND CLASS.						
0.0		SAN TOY		S 3.10							
4.1	D	SAYRE		A 3.35							
				P. M.							
		Time over Sub-division............ Average speed per hour............		0.25 9.8							

BALTIMORE AND OHIO
TIME TABLE NO. 29
Sunday May 28-1916
NEWARK DIVISION
NEWARK OHIO

EASTWARD.

	Train Order Stations.	New England Sub-Division. TIME-TABLE No. 29. May 28, 1916.	Passing Siding Capacity in Cars.	58 FRIDAY ONLY A. M.	SECOND CLASS.						
0.0	D	SAYRE		S10.25							
4.1		SAN TOY		A10.45							
				A. M.							
		Time over Sub-division............ Average speed per hour............		0.20 12.3							

Passenger trains will not exceed a speed of 15 miles per hour.
Speed as shown in Special Instruction 5, and such other restrictions as may be in effect, will not be exceeded.

G. W. GALLOWAY   GEN. MGR.
D. F. STEVANS   SUPT.
J. F. KEEGAN   GEN. SUPT.
J. R. KEARNEY   GEN. SUPT. TRANS.

CS&H Z&W train station, Shawnee, Ohio.

After arriving in Newark Yard, the Yard Master informed us to take the train to the coal yard, which was extreme east side. Coal was to be weighed and sent to Willard in late pm. Yes, all 40 loads coal was company fuel at Willard.

By the time we placed the engines on the inbound inspection pit, we were on duty and pay 15 hours and 55 minutes. Then register in with the Crew Dispatcher and head for home for some sleep and rest and wait on next call.

BRIDGE COLLAPSE ZANESVILLE DEC 5 - 1866

Bridge collapse, Zanesville, Ohio - Dec. 5, 1866.

Disasters on the Straitsville

There were many derailments and personal injuries to many employees. They operated the trains 24 hours a day and seven days a week, including all holidays, and in all kinds of weather and temperatures. The federal law stated that employees of trains could only on consecutive hours of 16. Before the law went into effect, there was no limit on the number of hours worked. The first known disaster was at Zanesville at the Muskingum River Bridge.

The following information is history secured from the Muskingum County collection. Although this happened before the Straitsville was built, there were many people from Perry, Licking and Franklin Counties on this train who were saved because their cars did not go in the river.

The Central Ohio Railroad Bridge Collapse

Although the Central Ohio Railroad bridge was built wide enough for a double track, only a single track was laid across the structure at first. A few days before the November 1853 opening of the bridge it had been tested by placing four locomotives with an aggregate weight of over 100 tons on the bridge at once. A Gazette editor wrote: *"For the passage of ordinary trains it may be considered quite as safe as any portion of the road."* When the first train crossed on November 10th *"...the weight of the train made not the slightest impression upon the bridge."*

By 1866 the double track across the bridge was in operation. This is the same year that the bankrupt Central Ohio became the Central Ohio Division of the Baltimore and Ohio Railroad. In the 13 years since the bridge was built, engines and cars had become much larger and heavier. This factor, in combination with the double track was to spell disaster.

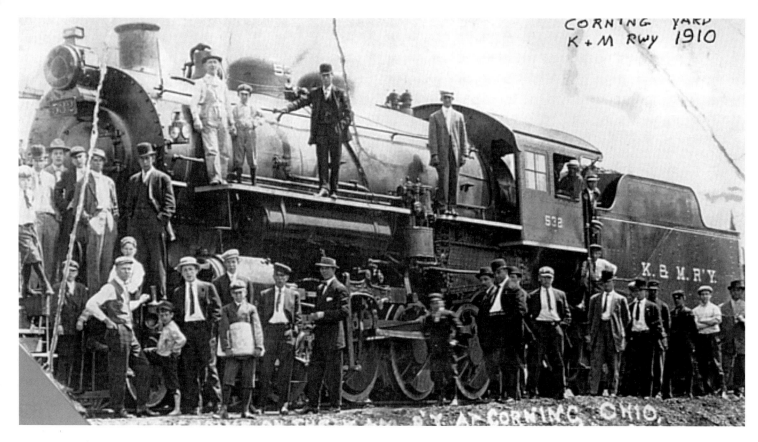

K&M Railway, new engine #532 at ready track, Corning, Ohio, 1910.

T&OC and K&W Round House, Corning, Ohio, Perry County, 1905.

A Central Ohio time table effective December 2, 1866 indicates that four passenger trains were crossing the Muskingum each day. There were two eastbound trains (Columbus to Bellaire), the No. 1 leaving Zanesville at 9:25 am, and No. 5 leaving here at 6:15 pm. The two westbound passenger trains (Bellaire to Columbus) were the No. 2 leaving Zanesville at 8:11 pm, and the No. 6 leaving at 8:00am. The No. 17 freight, leaving Zanesville bound for Columbus at 9:25 am, also carried passengers. This gave persons who had business in Columbus eight hours there and a chance to return home the same night. Other Central Ohio freight and work trains were also crossing the Muskingum Bridge at various intervals during the day.

On the night of December 4, 1866, a small Zanesville girl named Mary Winters had a dream that the Central Ohio Bridge had fallen into the river. The next morning, on the 5th at about 9:00, two westbound steam engines were crossing the bridge on the north track, (the westbound No. 6 passenger train had just safely crossed the bridge an hour before). One engine had just crossed the western-most span (span 4) and was on the western abutment with only its tender still on the bridge span. This first engine was soon followed by the second westbound yard engine pulling an empty car. The second engine had just started across span 4. At the same time, on the south track, the slow moving eastbound No. 1 morning passenger train from Columbus, consisting of four passenger cars, one baggage and one express car, was crossing the bridge. Its engine was just 20 feet from the pier at the east end of span 4, with the express and baggage cars on the span and a third car partially on the span. This train had just taken on wood and water at a point 100 yards west of the bridge.

The railroad had a rule that only one engine could be on any single span of the bridge at once. Just why this rule was not followed that morning is not known. The weight of all of these engines and cars on span 4, later estimated at 160 tons, caused the span to collapse into the river. Willard S. Pope describes the wreck scene:

When I reached the scene, the wreck was lying in the river undisturbed, and just as it fell. The general appearance was as follows: Two engines and the tender of the third and three cars were in the water. The remnants of the western-most (sic) car of the passenger train were lying at an angle with the track, as though it had been tipped over in falling. This, I learned, was in fact the case, as when the accident happened, only about half of the car was on the bridge, the rear truck being yet on the bank. The engines and the rest of the cars were standing upright on their wheels, almost exactly in the original line of their respective tracks. Lying on the tops of cars and engines were the chords and suspension bars, etc. of the two trusses of the bridge.

The noise made by the falling bridge, and especially by the hissing steam as the hot engines hit the water, could be heard for two miles. Within minutes, thousands of people crowded the river banks and were assisting in pulling people from the river. Fortunately the passenger car that was standing upright had been used as a smoking car, and only had a dozen passengers. Counting the train crews, a total of about 25 persons plummeted into the river.

The injured were taken to nearby houses. Only one individual was fatally hurt — Jesse Hill of Pleasant Valley, who suffered a fractured skull, badly cut arm, and internal injuries. Eight others suffered minor injuries. These individuals included James Haveland of Gaines Station, Michigan; Levi Claypool of Claypool's Mill along the Licking River; Mr. Milot, also of the Adams Express Company; Mr. Van Shipley, engineer of the yard engine; Silas Hakes (Hakas?), fireman of the yard engine; and Patrick H. Smith, engineer of the passenger train. Luckily the collapse of the span was slow enough that engineer Smith had time to sound a warning whistle, which alerted the brakeman. Although the express and baggage cars were in the water and the third car was standing on end resting on the baggage car, the last three cars of the train were stopped from falling 20 feet into the river. These latter cars were crowded with passengers.

The Baltimore and Ohio Railroad was very concerned about the cause of the bridge failure, since by this time the railroad had a number of these Bollman trusses in service. Willard Pope was civil engineer working for the Detroit Bridge and Iron Works. He was sent to Zanesville to examine the wreck and to determine the cause of the collapse for the bridge company and the railroad. He arrived at Zanesville on the evening of December 8th. By that time a temporary trestle had been erected to replace the collapsed span and maintain scheduled rail traffic, but the cars and engines, as well as the debris from the bridge span were still resting on the river bed, in six feet of water where they had fallen.

The wooden floor beams had been replaced a year and a half before the collapse, and Pope concluded that the collapse was caused by the weakness in the trussing under these floor beams, in combination with the heavier engines and cars. The design of this trussing had been altered from the original design by the railroad company. The Bollman Bridge was still considered an excellent one, and span 4 was soon replaced by another of the same style. The new span differed in a few minor details, however, including the use of cast iron end posts on the western abutment instead of stone blocks laid in cement used on the other spans.

It took three weeks to raise the engines from the river bed. Patrick Henry Rourke and his wrecking crane were called in from Baltimore when local crews failed to accomplish this task. Apparently there were so many B&O vice-presidents at the scent giving orders that nothing could be accomplished. In fact, Rourke was fired once for talking back to one of the officers, but rehired when additional attempts to raise the engines failed. When the job was finally completed, Rourke was fired again. He bought a lot and settled in Zanesville and earned a living splicing wire cables.

The first westbound engine with its tender still on the bridge when the span fell had been named the "Elias Fasset". The westbound yard engine was named ~Antelope". Built by Taunton Locomotive Works in Massachusetts, the 4-4-0 Antelope survived its plunge into the Muskingum, was renumbered Engine 523 by the B&O in 1867, and served on the Central Ohio Division until it was retired in 1873. The name and fate of the passenger train engine is not known.

An interesting sidelight to the bridge collapse was the fact that local residents were forced to cross the river via the Y bridge and pay the toll. They had been using the employee footwalk on the railroad bridge for many years to avoid this toll. Pressure on the legislators to buy the bridge soon mounted, but it was not until 1868 that the city council and county commissioners purchased the Y from the stockholders and removed the tolls.

Sat.29 - March-1924 - Locust Grove Disaster.

Shawnee freight goes thru bridge, four men are killed.

The following was secured from the Newark "Advocate" micro film collection.

Four trainmen were reported killed this morning, when the Shawnee local freight train crashed through the long bridge over Hog Run 5 miles Southwest of Newark.

At the B & O offices, it was said that the engine crew went down with the wreckage.

A report to the Fitzsimmons Brothers undertaking establishment said that four persons were dead.

The B & O wreck train and crew was hurried to the scene shortly after the report of the accident was received. The Shawnee passenger train was sent out behind the wreck train to act as a relief train. The engine crew included engineer E.M. Kastla and fireman Henry Gartner. Two brakeman were riding the engine. They were Ralph Powell and John Bidwell.

The train which met with disaster was Shawnee Local Freight No. 184 with Engine 2355. It is believed at the Newark offices of B & O Railroad that the heavy rain and high water this morning undermined the North bank and abutment under the bridge. This bridge is the first bridge South of Locust Grove Station.

The bridge apparently was all right when the train approached: when the engine on the bridge it collapsed, carrying the engine and crew in to the flood waters. Eight cars followed into and on top of engine.

This track is downgrade from Locust Grove to Hog Run. The train had 21 cars and caboose.

At the railroad offices it was stated that the water was high enough to cover the wreckage and it is feared that if the train crew escaped death in the crash that the men were drowned while pinned under the mass of crushed timbers and twisted iron. The train was the first since midnight to cross this bridge. At that time, the bridge had to be all right.

C.C. Larabee, conductor of the train was riding in caboose as was flagman Austin Oakleaf and two section men Frank Jurena and John Banzoskr.

The accident was reported, soon as possible, by conductor Larabee and arrangements made to rush assistance to the scene of the wreck. None of those who went down with the engine had been found at 11 a.m.

At 11:30 it was reported to B & O offices that the waters were receding and could see the tops of cars.

The following is a statement of Conductor Larabee: Mr. Farabee said he was riding in the caboose of the train with flagman Austin Oakleaf track foreman Frank Jurena and trackman John Banzoskr. The waters were high, they knew but Mr. Farabee stated that at Hog Run they were no higher than on many previous occasions, when the streams were swollen. He said that in dry season the stream is often without water. But nearby streams and springs caused it to rise rapidly.

The train was carrying 21 cars and had car loads of cinders to repair a washout at McCuneville.

After the crash came Mr. Farrabee and flagman ran to the front of disaster and found the engine enveloped in Hog Run and the 8 freight cars piled on top of it. They waited for a short time endeavoring to see if any of the men had jumped and cleared the wreck, but seeing no signs of life, they hurried to hunt a telephone. Conductor Farrabee stated that disaster consumed not more than five seconds. It was found hard to locate a telephone and they walked nearly a mile and tried five homes before they found one. Called the local B & O division offices to notify them of the catastrophe.

However, the local offices were aware that something unusual had happened.

The four men who so narrowly escaped were helpless to render any assistance to their comrades until the wreck train arrived on the scene.

Conductor Farabee said the accident Saturday was the first real trouble of any kind, that Mr. Kastla, the engineer was ever in. He had been in service with B & O since 1887. He had been engineer on Shawnee freight run for ten years.

Ralph Powell was the youngest man both in years and service. Was working the extra list for trainmen. The remainder of the crew were regular assigned and worked the train daily.

The location of the wreck, was almost inaccessible to motor cars, but a number of machines drove over flooded fields to reach the wreck. All efforts, were centered on the attempt to get the men from the wreckage, with faint hope, that somehow they might be living.

However, the accident happened at 8:50 a.m. and it was nearly 12 o'clock before the heavy debris was cleared away to reveal the bodies. Two were taken out, Powell and Gartner, the third was so located that it was sometime before it could be removed. Road foreman of engines R.A. (Dick) Vernon was actively engaged in the rescue work and went down into the wreckage at the water's edge to try and locate the bodies.

The bodies of Powell and Gartner were taken to Newark by train after 1 o'clock, a report at the B & O shops that a Frank Mahurd was on this train and was killed. This was not true, he board the first relief train out of Newark.

The bodies of Bidwell and Kastla were recovered late Saturday afternoon. Were taken by train to Newark. All the bodies were at funeral homes by Sunday and burial Tuesday.

The work of clearing the wreck, was as follows. All eight cars were pulled out and re-railed and sent to Newark shops. The heavy engine B & O 23S5 still rests in the creek bed of Hog Run.

Pile driver from Newark is driving pileing to form a temporary bridge. Foreman claim to have line open by Thursday. Building this bridge will allow wreck train crane approach near enough to lift the engine from creek.

The cause of this terrible wreck, was as follows: Officials of B & O with Superintendent H.G. Kruse met with H.M. Evans of P.U.C.O. and a McCauley of the I.C.C. all survivors of the train crew are to be interviewed. All men made a personal inspection of the wreck site. The trestle was rebuilt two years earlier. This section of bridge had never been affected by washouts. However on close inspection that small pockets had been washed out by the swift currents. This is in back of the bulkhead of bridge.

It is believed that the swift waters had caused an ~foundation at the approach to the trestle and as the weight of the engine passed over this, that the ground gave way allowing engine to drop. Bulkhead was pushed some but did not collapse. So, the cause of this wreck, was recorded: as excessive high water and swift currents causing wash out.   All four men met horrible deaths. I will not describe their fatal ending as was printed in the Advocate.   The bridge was rebuilt and the great railroad line to Shawnee reopened. This train wreck on this date Sat. 29- 1924 of March The Great Flood of 1913 happened the same date.

Newark, Ohio, April 5, 1924

Engine 2355 of the B&O Railroad was lifted and re-railed at Hog Run, Dutch Fork by the wreck train from Newark. The rail cars were pulled out first and returned to Newark shops. Engine 2355 has been taken to the car and engine shops at Newark. It will be rebuilt there.

Engine 2355 was a 2-8-0 freight engine, built by Baldwin Loco Work~, Philadelphia, Pennsylvania.

Temporary trestle has been pile driven in place by pile driver from Newark Division. Permanent bridge will be built later. After Engine 2355 was rebuilt i~ returned to service on the Newark. As for the bridge, it was rebuilt.

The large stone the B&O got to place in the wash out came from the Marrittia district of the OLK Division. To this date, the bridge is still being used by a scenic railway. The bridge has taken on many floods, but it has not washed out yet.

September 6, 1955

Was a member of B&O Lake Erie Local, switching rail cars at Mt. Vernon. We were in Cooper Bessemer weighing a car of scrap paper. When we were leaving and I was closing the gate, there was a explosion at the test building about 300 feet from me. I was blown backward about 10 feet against the chain link fence. I was only slightly injured. The east wall of the testing building was totally blown out. Three men were killed at once. I believe lady luck was with us because the scale was located about 50 feet from that test building.

The crew of this local train was as follows:

Richard Forbes - Engineer E. Merle Henry - Fireman Edward G. Welch - Conductor B. Morgan - Flagman Carl T. Winegarnder - Head Brakeman

Last Train from Newark
 By A. Harding Ganz
  55 Willowwood

A bit of Newark history passed almost unnoticed last Sunday afternoon. A few cars on East Main Street were inconvenienced as the railroad crossing lights began flashing, and clanging bells and harsh blare of the diesel air horn - two longs, a short and a long - signaled the advancing three engines and long train that clattered and bumped out of the B&O Newark Yard at First Street and rumbled northward out of town. It was the last time that a train would originate from the Newark railroad yard.

Symbol freight train WI-35, destination the big junction at Willard in northern Ohio, had formed down on Track Five in the B&O Yard, from cuts of cars switched from local industries. Three big diesels were lashed-up at the head end, colorful in their yellow, orange and blue markings and sporting the Chessie kitten herald, two General Motors ''Geeps'' or "G.P.'s (for General Purpose) and a General Electric "U-boat".

The engines idled while the car inspector checked the air brake hoses of the consist, 71 cars, more than usual. WI-35 was then cleared to proceed as "Extra Forty-two Fifty-five West." David Stidham, crewing as fireman, opened the throttle of the lead engine, B&O 4255, and the three units began to throb more forcefully, moving forward, taking up slack in the couplings. Brakeman Bob Taft set the switches as the train moved out of the yard, the freight car wheels squealing and groaning on the iron rails.

The train growled slowly across the bridge spanning the fast-flowing North Fork of the Licking River, across the Conrail main line at the interlocking signal and northward up the east leg of the Wye track. As the lead engine passed the brick B&O yard office at First Street, radio call sign "WF", Engineer Joe Holley and Conductor Carl Winegardner reached for the grab irons and swung aboard. They carried overnight bags and thermoses, and the conductor had a wad of train orders given him by Caller-Operator Walter Dorsey. Flagman John Young rode the blue B&O bay-window caboose, completing the five-man train crew. It was about 2:20pm when the head-end diesels blared their way across East Main and East Church streets and then under the Route 16 overpass, heading north, stretching out to three-quarters of a mile long.

By the time relief Call-Operator John Degenhart arrived, WI-35 had passed well beyond Newark and Vanatta, paralleling Route 13 toward Mt. Vernon and Mansfield. From now on WI-35 would originate from Chessie's Parsons Yard in south Columbus. It will pass through Newark, three days a week as before, but now only to set off or pick up blocks of cars. And the return run, NK-36, will be renamed PA-36. Other Conrail and Chessie trains will continue to set off the local grade crossing signals, and the B&O Yard will still see cuts of cars shunted back and forth. But March 3, 1985, was the last day a train originated from Newark.

On the following day, March 4, 1985, this same crew returned to Newark with train NK-36. This being the last Benwood, West Virginia train. After train BW-98 arrived in Benwood, the railroad from Lamira to Gibson was shut down.

The Lake Erie train from Columbus to Willard and return only lasted a short period of time. Then this railroad from Butler to Mansfield Bowman street was shut down. After this shut down, this prevented any through trains. After a short period of time, Butler to Fredericktown was also shut down. The Central Ohio Line was totally shut down from Lamira to Bellaire, and the River Bridge sold to Wheeling and Lake Erie. All of this happened in the 1980's. Now what is left of the B&O line is Newark to Gibson and Newark to Fredericktown, 1996.

88

Basketball Glenford's Teams

Back in 1907 the Board of Education granted approval for the school to floor its first cage team. Although the facts surrounding that first contest have disappeared into the past, it is known that the late A. B. Long of Newark, a nationally known athletic official, hitched up his horse and buggy and made the overnight trip to Glenford to referee the conflict. His pay as a gallon of maple syrup, which on the basis of today's pay scale was rather good pay in those days.

The contest marked the beginning of a long and illustrious basketball career for the Glenford community. There are so many stories about basketball teams in Glenford over these many years that, if we tried to tell them all, we could fill an entire book on them alone. Each player on all of the teams could go on for hours once he gets started. It would be unfair to quote some of these stories and leave others out; therefore, this will be a rather general outline of our basketball history here in Glenford.

At one time during the 1900's our teams played upstairs in the old Glenford High School. In 1921 the first Perry County tournament was played here with Crooksville winning the title. When the new high school was built in 1930-31, games moved across the street. We can remember seeing a line of fans from the front door of the high school, down both sets of steps and out to the street, all waiting to see a game. Some can even remember when they came on the trains to see a game. In 1956 the new Glen ford Elementary was completed, and it was here that Glenford basketball finished out its great history.

Between 1925 and 1960 Glenford High School won ten district titles. This is a record for Class "A" teams in modern history, dating back to 1923. The Glenford "Golden Horde" also took the State Championship title in 1941. Previous to the organization tournament in 1923, the school competed on equal terms in the old state tournament held at Ohio Wesleyan University, Delaware, Ohio. In this event Glen ford knocked off Dayton Steele in 191 5, and sports writers, covering the event, were still trying to find out a week later where the Glenford team came from. Glenford went to the Class "B" State Tournament in 1925. Glenford's basketball fortunes probably moved into prominence around 1939, when the school for three straight years sent teams into the state tournament. In 1939 the school was knocked off in the state quarter-finals by Sandusky St. Mary's 40-33. In 1 940 Glenford lost to Canfield 50-45 in the semi-finals. In 1941 it was a different story when the team trounced Canfield in the championship game 48-28.

Playing a prominent part in that three-year surge was Dick Shrider, now Athletic Director at Miami University in Oxford, Ohio. In 1939 he was named on the All-Ohio second team. In 1940 he was named to the All-Ohio team and was a member of the first team in all tournaments up to and including the 1941 state championship event. He made the Associated Press All-Ohio team in 1940 and was high scorer in the county, district, and state tourneys. He scored 604 points in the 33 games for one season's record. Other Glenford basketball players gaining state recognition were Herb Shrider and Glen Hursey.

Herb Shrider, captain of the 1939-40 team, was named All Ohio Center in 1939. He was also the leading scorer for his team that season. He was named to the first All District tournament team in 1940.

Glen Hursey is the only Class "A" (then Class "B") player in Ohio to make the All State team 3 years in a row. Hursey did this in 1946, '47, and '48.

Don Rushing, coach at Glenford from 1951 to 1960, was named Ohio High School Class "A" Basketball Coach of the Year in 1958. There is no record of another Perry County coach being named Ohio coach of the year. Glenford Golden Horde was rated the No. 1 club in its division during the 1958 season, but lost to Buchtel in the district play off. Up through 1958 Rushing's teams had won 160 games and lost only 19. Also during that period Glenford was league champions 6 years and tournament champs for 4 years (1953, '54, '56, and '58). Dewey Barr co-captain of the 1952 and '53 team was named all Ohio center in 1953. Jim Hamilton was named all Ohio guard in 1956.

Glenford's final basketball team of 1960, coached by Don Rushing, closed out the school records with a fine season. They finished with a regular season record of 16-4. They lost to Corning 63-58 in the finals of the Perry County Tournament, but they came back to beat Corning 61-55 in the District finals. They defeated Granville in the regional tournament 45-42, but lost to New Boston 49-41 in the finals.

Glenford holds the record in Perry County for winning the District 10 times. Perry County holds the record for the only county to win the State Championship two years in a row—Glenford in 1941 and Somerset in 1942. New Lexington St. Aloysius took the State Title in 1954, making a total of three Perry County teams to win the State Championship.

1941 State Champions.

Glenford trips to regional and state tournaments:

1925—Coach Byron Foucht—Glenford lost to state Champions, Bellpoint, 35-12, in semi-finals.

1939—Coach Nolan Swackhammer—Glenford defeated Amanda 40-37, but lost to Sandusky St. Mary's 40-33 in semi-finals.

1940—Coach Nolan Swackhammer—Glenford defeated Amanda 43-40 and Rittman 46-32, but lost to Canfield 50-45 in semi-finals.

1941—Coach Nolan Swackhammer—Glenford defeated defending State Champions, Canfield 48 28 to win the State Championship.

1945—Coach Jack McClain—Glenford defeated Sugar Creek 48-44 but lost to Ashville 41-36 in regional finals at Logan.

1946—Coach Jack McClain—Glenford lost to Worthington 34-32 in regionals at Athens.

1948—Coach Bill Ross—Glenford defeated Bremen 61 -36 and Lucasville 50-31 at Athens regional; lost to Eaton 45-43 in state semi-finals.

1953—Coach Don Rushing—Glenford defeated Williamsport 68-55 and then lost to Philo 82-67 in regional finals.

1956—Coach Don Rushing—Glenford lost to New Boston 67-61 in regional opener at Athens.

1960—Coach Don Rushing—Glenford defeated Granville 45-42 but lost to New Boston 49-41 in regional semi-finals.

PERRY COUNTY TOURNAMENT WINNERS

YEAR	FIRST	SECOND	YEAR	FIRST	SECOND
1921	Crooksville	Thornville	1945	Glenford	Shawnee
1922	No Tournament due to the Flu		1946	Corning	Glenford
			1947	Corning	Glenford
1923	New Straitsville	Crooksville	1948	Glenford	Junction City
1924	Glenford	Somerset	1949	Junction City	Thornville
1925	Glenford	Somerset	1950	Junction City	Corning
1926	Glenford	New Straitsville	1951	Corning	Shawnee
1927	Glenford	Thornville	1952	Corning	Glenford
1928	Hemlock	McLuney	1953	Glenford	Somerset
1929	Glenford	Thornville	1954	Glenford	Junction City
1930	New Lexington	Glenford	1955	Junction City	Thornville
1931	Shawnee	Glenford	1956	Glenford	Somerset
1932	Shawnee	Thornville	1957	Corning	Shawnee
1933	Junction City	Corning	1958	Glenford	Somerset
1934	Thornville	Shawnee	1959	Corning	Somerset
1935	Junction City	Glenford	1960	Coming	Glenford
1936	Glenford	Junction City			
1937	Shawnee	Glenford			
1938	Shawnee	Moxahala			
1939	Glenford	Shawnee			
1940	Shawnee	Glenford			
1941	Glenford	Somerset			
1942	Somerset	Corning			
1943	Thornville	Corning			
1944	Glenford	Corning			

Glenford won district tournaments in 1925, 1939, 1940, 1941, 1945, 1946, 1948, 1953, 1956, and 1960.

PERRY COUNTY TOURNAMENT RECORDS

Most Championships: Glenford—15 Years: 1924, '25, '26, '27, '29, '36, 1939, '41, '44, '45, '48, '53, '54, '56, and 1958. Next is Corning with 7. Most times in Finals: Glenford — 26. Next are Shawnee and Corning with 11.

Widest Point Margin in Title Game: 1948 — 24 points (Glenford 73, Junction City 49).
Widest Point Margin in any Game: 1956 — 59 points (Glenford 1 05, Moxahala 47).
Most Combined Points in Title Game: 1958 — 162 points (Glenford 83, Somerset 79).
Most Combined Points in any Game: 1958 — 162 points (Glenford 82, Somerset 79).
Fewest Combined Points in Title Game: 1927 — 22 points (Glenford 13, Thornville 9).
Fewest Combined Points in any Game: 1924 — 1 5 points (Junction City 12, New Straitsville 3).
Fewest Points for Winner in Title Game: 1927 — 13 points (Glenford 13, Thornville 9).
Fewest Points for Winner in any Game: 1924 — 1 2 points (Junction City 1 2, New Straitsville 3).
Most Points for Winner in Title Game: 1958 — 83 points (Glenford 83, Somerset 79).
Most Points for Winner in any Game: 1956 — 105 points (Glenford 105, Moxahala 47).
Fewest Points for Loser in Title Game: 1927 — 9 points (Glenford 13, Thornville 9).
Fewest Points for Loser in any Game: 1924 — 3 points (Junction City 12, New Straitsville 3).
Most Field Goals in Title Game: 1958 — 34 field goals (Glenford 83, Somerset 79).
Most Field Goals in any Game: 1956 — 45 field goals (Glenford 105, Moxahala 47).
Most Free Throws Made in Title Game: 1953 — 23 free throws—Glenford (Glenford 69, Somerset 48).

SEASON RECORD OF THE 1941 STATE CHAMPS
Glenford—1941—(30-2)

Glenford	59	Junction City	32
Glenford	40	Somerset	28
Glenford	48	Thornville	24
Glenford	55	Shawnee	28
Glenford	67	New Lexington	32
Glenford	33	Corning	43
Glenford	66	Hemlock	32
Glenford	28	Lancaster St. Mary	31
Glenford	41	New Straitsville	23
Glenford	54	Junction City	32
Glenford	42	Somerset	38
Glenford	55	Lancaster St. Mary	29
Glenford	67	Shawnee	39
Glenford	46	Philo	41
Glenford	48	Ashville	25
Glenford	53	Corning	41
Glenford	65	Moxahala	28
Glenford	54	Thornville	24
Glenford	57	Philo	43
Glenford	68	McLuney	18
Glenford	48	Canfield	28

INDIVIDUAL RECORDS

Most Points in Championship Game: 1953—32 points—Dewey Barr, Glenford (Glenford vs. Somerset).
Most Free Throws in Championship Game: 1953— 12 free throws—Dewey Barr, Glenford (Glenford vs. Somerset). Record for Most Points in District: 1948—51 points —Glen Hursey (Glenford vs. Somerset). 1941—50 points—Richard Shrider (Glenford vs. Mercerville).

CHAMPIONSHIP BOX SCORE

GLENFORD	FG	FT	T	CANFIELD	FG	FT	T
Axline	1	3	5	Miskell	0	2	2
Noyles	0	0	0	Sloan	0	0	0
Hollister	6	3	15	Hendricks	1	1	3
Shrider	8	1	17	Bunts	0	0	0
Lattimer	0	0	0	Cummings	6	2	14
Schofield	4	1	9	McPhee	2	0	4
Cotterman	0	0	0	Hedge	1	0	2
Henderson	1	0	2	Zimmerman	0	1	1
Swinehart	0	0	0	Greer	0	0	0
				Evans	1	0	2
TOTALS	20	8	48	TOTALS	11	6	28

GLENFORD	14	28	38	48
CANFIELD	5	9	20	28
OFFICIALS:	Martin Bishop and H.C. Campbell			

COUNTY TOURNEY

Glenford	52	Corning	29
Glenford	82	McLuney	28
Glenford	72	Moxahala	29
Glenford	69	Junction City	39

DISTRICT TOURNEY

Glenford	84	Mercerville	17
Glenford	53	Ames Bern	19
Glenford	49	Racine	31
Glenford	60	Rome Stewart	20

FIRST ROUND

Hicksville	38	Spring Valley	37
Glenford	51	Smithville	41
Elmore	37	Berlin Twp.	35
Xenia OSSO	42	Loudenville	32
Attica	34	Hamilton Hanover	46
Midvale	42	Watterloo	37
Criderville	48	Fairfield Twp.	46

QUARTERFINALS

Glenford	37	Hicksville	33
Xenia OSSO	27	Elmore	23
Canfield	48	Hamilton Hanover	42
Midvale	30	Cridersville	23

SEMI-FINALS

Glenford	45	Xenia OSSO	35
Canfield	44	Midvale	36

1958 Team—1st Row *L-R:* Bill Hill, Darrell Gutridge, Tom Denison, Ronnie King, Richard Wilkins, Leroy Parsons, Coach Don Rushing, Ronnie Gordon, John Skinner, Donald Fisher, Jan Bryan, Charles Morehead, Henry Taylor, Carl Gutridge, Dean Kroft.

1960 Team—1st Row L-R Coach Don Rushing, Ronald Gordon, Carl Gutridge, John Cotterman, Larry Shrider. Tom Denison. *2nd Row:* Harold Gutridge, Donald Fisher, Charles Morehead, Tom Shater, Leroy Parsons, John Skinner. Duane Hupp.

Cheerleaders—L-R Charlene Henderson Hill, Arlene Mack Hill, Bonnie Smith Goldsberry, Kay Starkey Springer.

EFFECT 12:30 AM CST WEST BOUND TRAINS. MONDAY JUNE 2-1890 SM&N

PASSENGER TRAINS—First Class.   FREIGHT TRAINS—Second Class.

NO. 5.	NO. 57.	NO. 9.	NO. 17.	NO. 7.	NO. 3.	NO. 47.	NO. 15.	STATIONS.	NO. 23.	NO. 25.	NO. 31.	NO. 2.	NO. 29.	NO. 59.	NO. 23.
		Pass'gr. Daily exc't Sunday.	Pass'gr. Daily.	Limited. Daily.	Passenger. Daily.	Express. Daily exc'pt Monday.	Passenger. Daily exc'pt sunday.		Quick Disp. Freight. Daily.	Freight. Daily.	Way Freight Daily exc't Sunday.	Freight. Daily.	Freight. Daily.	Quick Disp. Freight. Daily.	Freight. Daily.
AM Ar	AM Ar	AM Ar	PM Ar	PM Ar	PM Ar	PM Ar	PM Ar		AM Ar	PM Ar	PM Ar	PM Ar	AM Ar	AM Ar	AM Ar
		9.10	12.30		6.35			Sandusky		2.45	4.50		1.35	3.45	6.40
		9.04	12.24		6.31			L. S. & M. S. Crossing		2.40	4.45		1.32	3.30	6.35
		9.01	12.18		6.25			Perkins'		2.27	4.32		1.16	3.24	6.16
		8.55	12.12		6.18			Prout's		2.10 / 2.00	4.17		1.05	3.14	6.04
		8.50	12.07PM		6.12			Higbee		1.53	4.05		12.55	3.03	5.52
		8.42	11.59AM		6.02			Roby's Siding		1.35	3.45		12.37	2.43	5.33
	2.15	8.31	11.53 / 11.45		6.01			Monroeville		1.23	3.44 / 3.31		12.35	2.40	5.31
	2.03	8.31	11.37		5.51			Pontiac		1.16	4.05		12.20	2.25	5.15
	1.57	8.27	11.29		5.43			Havana		1.00	4.50		12.05AM	2.10	5.00
	1.49	8.20	11.22		5.35			Centerton		12.45	4.33		11.50PM	1.55	4.43
3.10	1.43	8.05 / 8.00	11.14	1.45	5.30 / 5.10	9.55	11.40	Chicago Junction	8.30	12.40 / 12.35	4.25 / 4.10	5.00	11.40 / 11.00	1.45 / 1.35	4.35
	3.00	7.53	11.12	1.36	5.03	9.48	11.31	New Haven	8.17	12.25	12.58	4.48	10.47	1.20	4.23
	2.55	7.46	11.06	1.33	4.56	9.43	11.24	Plymouth	8.04	12.10PM	12.45	4.36	10.21 / 10.21	1.05	4.08
3.23		7.40	11.00	1.26	4.49	9.37	11.16	Forest	7.51	11.57AM	12.30	4.24	10.06	12.50	3.51
3.13		7.39	10.52	1.21	4.40	9.20	11.07	Shelby Junction	7.32 / 7.22	11.41	12.01PM	4.06	9.48	12.25	2.31 / 2.03
		7.30	10.50	1.19	4.36	9.27	11.05	Shelbytown	7.10	11.38	11.55AM	4.02	9.44	12.20AM	3.00
3.05		7.20	10.40	1.11	4.26	9.19	10.55	Spring Mill	6.51	11.15	11.30	3.37 / 3.27	9.19 / 9.08	11.55PM	2.30 / 2.20
2.55		7.10	10.31	1.04	4.16	9.11	10.43	North Siding	6.31	10.55	11.10	3.04	8.43 / 8.33	11.36	2.00
2.53		7.04	10.29	1.02	4.14	9.00	10.41	Mansfield	6.27	10.40	11.04	2.50	8.25	11.31	1.56
2.40		6.54	10.20	12.53	4.00	9.00	10.30	Alta	6.10	10.20 / 9.45	10.40	2.40	7.55	11.15 / 11.05	1.40
2.40		6.50	10.12	12.45	3.50	8.52	10.22	Lexington	5.45	9.19	10.12 / 10.02	2.00	7.00	10.53	1.10
2.33		6.42	10.04	12.37	3.40	8.44	10.13	Shaffer's Siding	5.25	8.56	9.45	1.37	6.32 / 6.22	10.13 / 10.03	12.45
2.31		6.40	10.03	12.36	3.39	8.43	10.11	Belleville	5.20	8.52	9.42	1.33	6.15	9.56	12.40
2.28		6.31	9.50	12.33	3.34	8.40	10.06	Glover's	5.11	8.44	9.35	1.23	6.07	9.48	12.30
2.23		6.20	9.52	12.26	3.27	8.35	9.58	Independence	4.57	8.30	9.25	1.05	5.54 / 5.40	9.36 / 9.20	12.10AM
2.11		6.15	9.41	12.20	3.16	8.27	9.47	Ankenytown	4.39 / 4.22	8.06	8.52	12.30 / 12.10PM	5.00 / 4.30	8.40	11.42 / 11.33PM
2.07		6.04	9.31	12.13	3.07	8.20	9.38	Frederick	4.00 / 3.30	7.47	8.29	11.44AM	3.50 / 3.10	8.00	11.13
1.53		5.52	9.17	12.02PM	2.59	8.09	9.23	Mt. Vernon	3.07	7.20	8.00 / 7.35	11.17 / 10.55	3.15	7.10	10.55
1.45		5.41	9.05	11.52AM	2.40	7.50	9.10	Hunt's	2.42	6.55	7.13	10.23	2.45	7.10 / 6.50	10.32 / 10.14
1.37		5.31	8.53	11.45	2.29	7.51	8.50	Utica	2.16	6.35	6.55	10.05	2.00 / 2.10	6.21	9.55
1.30		5.22	8.46	11.38	2.19	7.44	8.40	St. Louisville	1.55	6.17	6.30	9.30	1.40	5.55	9.11
1.25		5.16	8.40	11.31	2.13	7.36	8.42	Vanatta's	1.40	6.05	6.15	9.15	1.37	5.40 / 5.30	8.57
1.19		5.00	8.33	11.25	2.04	7.30	8.34	Kibler's Siding	1.20	5.30	5.56	8.55	1.20	5.00	8.35
1.15		5.33	8.30	11.20	2.00	7.22	8.30	Newark	1.15	5.25	5.50	8.50	1.15	4.50	8.30
AM Lv	AM Lv	AM Lv	AM Lv	AM Lv	AM Lv	PM Lv	PM Lv		AM Lv	AM Lv	AM Lv	AM Lv	PM Lv	PM Lv	PM Lv
NO. 5.	NO. 57.	NO. 9.	NO. 17.	NO. 7.	NO. 3.	NO. 47.	NO. 15.								

BALTIMORE AND OHIO   SANDUSKY MANSFIELD AND NEWARK